SCHOLASTIC

Scaffolded Writing Instruction

Teaching With a Gradual-Release Framework

Douglas Fisher and Nancy Frey

NEW YORK • TORONTO • LONDON • AUCKLAND • SYDNEY
MEXICO CITY • NEW DELHI • HONG KONG • BUENOS AIRES

Teaching *Resources*

For Bridget, Devin, Eric, and Liz

Pages 51 and 52: Charts adapted from "Responders Are Taught, Not Born" in the *Journal of Adolescent and Adult Literacy*. Copyright 2003 © by J. Simmons. Used by permission of the publisher.

Page 58: Speaking Checklist adapted from "An Integrated Approach to the Teaching and Assessment of Language Arts." In S. R. Hurley & J. V. Tinajero (eds.), *Literacy assessment of second language learners*. Copyright © 2001 by D. Lapp, D. Fisher, J. Flood, and A. Cabello. Reprinted with permission of Allyn & Bacon.

Page 116: Stanzas for an "I Am" Poem from "Writing Instruction for Struggling Adolescent readers: A Gradual Release Model" in the *Journal of Adolescent and Adult Literacy*. Copyright © 2003 by the authors. Used by permission of the publisher.

Page 124: Story Pyramid template from "Writing Models: Strategies for Writing Composition in Inclusive Settings." *Reading & Writing Quarterly*. Copyright © 2001 by L. A. Stahl. Used by permission of the publisher.

Chapter 8: Adapted from "A Picture Prompts a Thousand Words: Creating Photo Essays With Struggling Writers" in *California English*. Copyright © 2003 by Nancy Frey. Used by permission of the publisher.

Edited by Sarah Glasscock

Cover design by Maria Lilja

Interior design by Melinda Belter

ISBN-13 978-0-439-69649-4

ISBN-10 0-439-69649-6

3 4 5 6 7 8 9 10   40   14 13 12

Contents

Introduction

In reading, we've been taught to decode and comprehend. We've also been taught to respond and react to texts. Can we say the same for writing? Most of us have been taught to encode and spell, but have we been taught to create and react to writing? The answer is most likely no. We have been assigned writing tasks, mostly in the form of independent writing prompts, but we haven't been taught to write or to respond to our own writing. The question, then, is how do we teach our students to write? But before we answer that question, let's answer a more basic question—why should we write?

Why Should We Write?

In their article, "What Reading Does for the Mind" (1998), Anne Cunningham and Keith Stanovich note, "Reading has cognitive consequences that extend beyond its immediate task of lifting meaning from a particular passage." They suggest that reading volume has implications for vocabulary expansion, development of background knowledge, understanding of text structures, and increasing verbal skills. Cunningham and Stanovich use the term "Matthew effect," taken from the Biblical passage that describes the rich getting richer and the poor getting poorer, to describe the phenomenon that students who read more are better readers. Naturally, not all reading is equal, and it is important for students to read material that either matches their reading level or is highly motivating.

Writing is the flip side of this same coin. Students who are taught to write and who write often will write more, and in many cases, better. Our work suggests that there is also a Matthew effect in writing: Writers who are given time to write and who receive instruction and feedback become richer. That is, they write more because they have more opportunities to do so. However, this is not the same as saying that their writing automatically becomes better. Sheer volume is not the same as quality writing.

Unfortunately, students are often given writing assignments, but they receive little systematic instruction. In this case, practice does not make perfect. Instead, as our colleague Leif Fearn often points out, practice makes permanent. We need to guide students carefully as their writing repertoires become permanent.

We know that writing does good things for students' minds. Writing allows them to think in different ways, explore issues, learn new content, and share what they know. In other words, *writing is thinking*. Consider the following example from a fifth-grade classroom:

The students in Ms. Aida Allen's class are members of book clubs. The class is divided into several small groups or clubs, with each group reading a different book. For this round of books, Ms. Allen has selected different books to spur discussion in which the main character changes over time. Tino's group is reading *Shiloh* by Phyllis Naylor. It's the story of Marty, a young boy who befriends an abused dog. Ms. Allen wants her students to write a character analysis as the culminating activity. She asks Tino, "How has Marty changed since we first met him in chapter one?" In response, Tino answers, "I don't know yet ... I haven't written in my journal." (You'll read more about Ms. Allen's class in the following pages.)

Tino's assertion is supported by research on expert writers conducted by J. R. Hayes. He found that "the content of the sentence may not be fully determined before the writer begins to produce syntactically complete sentence parts." In other words, even expert writers found that they constructed meaning *while* they wrote. This process is often called "writing to learn." Teachers can use writing as a way to encourage thinking because it provides students with time to discover what it is they think, and not just to record their thoughts.

We also know that *writing and reading are related*. Leif Fearn and Nancy Farnan have noted that there are significant *interactions* between reading and writing. Timothy Shanahan has discovered that writing impacts students' learning to read. Other researchers, such as M. A. K. Halliday, have suggested that all learning is language based. As humans, we listen, read, and view to obtain information. We speak, write, and create to share information. Our species is the only one that stores information outside of our bodies. In order to store this information, we must convert it into a code that can be readily translated by other members of the species. The common denominator is the fact that we want to exchange information with one another.

Teachers certainly want to do this, but so do young people who visit chat rooms and converse on cell phones. The goal is to transfer a message from one person to the other; the way we do that is through speaking, listening, reading, writing, and viewing. The code we use is our oral and written language. Unless we develop the ability to mentally telegraph messages or read minds, we must rely on our literacy skills to make our needs and wants known.

Another way of thinking about the interaction between reading and writing was suggested to us by Leif Fearn. In a seminar, he pointed out that teachers can spend a significant amount of time teaching students to read— but they may never become good writers. However, if teachers focused on writing instruction, students would become good readers. We all know readers who can't write, but do we know writers who can't read?

In the early 1970s, three people were beginning to focus on writing instruction—Donald Murray, Janet Emig, and Donald Graves. As Don Graves said in a 2002 interview in *The California Reader*, "I'm not saying that reading isn't important, but that's only one wing to make the plane fly. You've got to have two wings. There is so much reading in writing. Kids who are writers read differently because they are in the construction business, making texts themselves."

Again we ask ourselves, this time with even more fervor, "How do we teach our students to write?" One common approach has been to rely on the writing process. We feel that there are pitfalls in focusing solely on one process.

The Writing Process

Proponents of the writing process suggest that writers use five steps to produce a piece of completed writing: prewriting, writing, revising, editing, and publishing. Given any genre or writing task, a student in a writing-process classroom will be instructed to engage in the five steps in sequential order. At its extreme, the daily activities might look like this.

MONDAY	TUESDAY	WEDNESDAY	THURSDAY	FRIDAY
Prewriting	Writing	Revising	Editing	Publishing

While there are a number of very positive aspects to understanding the writing process, there are also some significant limitations. We introduced Donald Murray, Janet Emig, and Donald Graves earlier; they are often recognized as the instigators of the writing process. As Don Graves pointed out in the interview mentioned previously, Donald Murray was the first person to use the term "writing process." However, Graves goes on to say, "We abandoned the term because all kinds of distortions came in of what is really an artful process. It got all messed up by all the interpretations people were giving it. When I heard that people were using the five- or seven-step 'Graves' writing process, I flipped out." Graves knows that writing is much more complex than a simple, linear process.

While the originators of the idea realized that a lock-step focus on the writing process is misguided, there are hundreds of workshops, professional books, and Internet sites devoted to the idea. We would feel more comfortable if their term were "writing processes." Given the current focus on "the writing process," let's explore a few reasons why this idea can be problematic.

First, real writers don't write like that. Writing is a recursive, not a linear, process. Writers edit as they think about what they write. They revise during their writing and brainstorm (or prewrite) as they edit. A study of proficient writers found that they rarely produced whole sentences while writing (Kaufer, Hayes, and Flower, 1986). Instead, they created sentence parts, separated by pauses of a second or two, which were then strung together to form a complete sentence. The more expert the writer, the longer the average sentence part they wrote. According to research by Kaufer, Hayes, and Flower, the best writers wrote an average of 11.2 words before pausing. And Hayes has found that most commonly, good writers reread as they wrote *each sentence part* and made changes based on syntactical or semantic evaluations of their writing. In fact, most professional writers will say that they don't have one single process they use—they use different processes depending on the writing task, the amount of time they have, and their audience.

Second, as teachers, we know that not all pieces need to be published. Some writing, such as journal or diary entries, is personal. We don't want or need students to prewrite, revise, and edit this work. Similarly, other writing is intended as a knowledge check. We use writing-to-learn prompts, such as *write about how you solved the math problem*, to determine if students

Traditional Writing Process Model	Real Writing
• writers follow a single, linear process	• writers use many processes to achieve different goals
• publication is always the goal	• there are many goals for writing, including but not limited to publication
• process is neat, organized into five progressive stages	• process is recursive and flows in many directions as writers go back and forth between prewriting, drafting, revising, and editing

understand content. We wouldn't want to spend time using the writing process to find out this information. When students are taught to think that writing must occur in five sequential steps, they often believe that every piece must be revised, edited, and published. This is false. It causes them, and us, to miss opportunities to write for writing's sake.

Third, the writing process doesn't provide teachers with information on their instructional role. When, for example, should a teacher teach mechanics and conventions (spelling, grammar, and so on) or thesis development? Should that type of instruction come during prewriting, editing, or revising? Should the whole class receive instruction on a specific topic when a few students make errors? Or should teachers provide instruction before students make errors?

Knowing that there are processes, whether in reading or writing, does not mean that instruction should be directly linked to each of those processes in isolation of the others. Let's think about this in terms of reading processes. Do we divide up class time and spend a day on grapheme/phoneme relationships, another day on syntax and grammar, and then a third day on comprehension? We hope not! Instead, we teach students how to integrate these processes by modeling their use in authentic tasks. We teach students to use different strategies when they come to words they don't know or a section of text they don't understand.

Our experience suggests that writing processes should be treated the same way. Students need to know that there are commonalities and differences in the processes writers use. They must learn what to do when they are stuck. Students must also learn that all writing is recursive, interactive, involves a lot of reading, and is somewhat messy.

We don't believe that writers are born. Instead, we believe that writers are created. They're created when teachers nurture their development and provide focused instruction and feedback. In writing instruction we've found that a systematic approach, rather than a rigid, lock-step approach, increases students' performance in writing (and by extension, reading). In the following chapters, we provide an overview of the gradual release framework for writing instruction, discuss how to assess students' needs and progress, and then present an in-depth discussion of each approach in the framework and how to incorporate it in your classroom.

An Overview of the Gradual-Release Instructional Framework

Think of your favorite book. What makes that particular book so important to you? What did the writer do to capture your interest in such a significant way? If Doug had been asked to answer that question in fifth grade, he would have chosen *The Children's Story* because the author James Clavell made him feel like he was right there in a post-war classroom. If Nancy had the opportunity to answer this question during her childhood, she would have selected *The Secret Garden* because the writer Frances H. Burnett combined suspense, great dialogue, and fascinating characters.

Now think about your own writing. What is your best piece of work? For most of us, that's a much harder question to answer. We believe this is because we haven't been taught to write like we've been taught to read.

Our gradual-release instructional framework for writing instruction seeks to combine the best components of two practices—scaffolded approaches for teaching writing skills and strategies and the writing workshop model. This framework unifies purposeful, needs-based instruction with the processes of writing. Instruction is conducted systematically using the full range of resources in the classroom, including teacher-directed instruction, guided practice, collaboration with peers, and independent application.

As we'll discuss in greater detail in the section that follows, the use of a gradual release of responsibility framework ensures that writers are created, nurtured, and cultivated in the classroom. At its heart, writing instruction matters because it teaches children to think about and respond to their world. Is there a greater purpose in education?

The Gradual Release of Responsibility Framework for Writing Instruction

The gradual release of responsibility stipulates that the teacher moves from assuming "all the responsibility for performing a task ... to a situation in which the students assume all of the responsibility" (Duke & Pearson, 2004). This gradual release may occur over a day, a week, a month, or a year.

Michael Graves and Bonnie Graves also write that "effective instruction often follows a progression in which teachers gradually do less of the work and students do more. It is through this process of gradually assuming more responsibility for their learning that students become competent, independent learners."

In a gradual release of responsibility instructional framework, the teacher first models the desired learning. Over time, students assume more responsibility for the task as they move from participants in modeled lessons, to apprentices in shared instruction, to collaborators with their peers, to independent performers. The chart on page 12 describes each instructional approach we use and shows the shifting level of support required from teachers as students perform increasingly independent writing tasks.

The framework should not be interpreted as a strict hierarchy, in which you teach each approach for a designated period of time until all students "reach" independent writing. Rather we have identified seven approaches that target different areas of a writer's development and support different writing processes. Each requires different degrees of support from the teacher. Most, like Power Writing, a fluency-building approach, are revisited daily or weekly to sharpen skills and teach new aspects of writing. Others, like LEA, a sentence and vocabulary-building approach that best supports struggling writers, may be utilized only occasionally. It all depends on the needs of your students as evidenced in assessments of their performance, a topic we discuss in Chapter 2.

What does this mean for writing instruction? Understanding the gradual release of responsibility framework means that you cannot simply assign more writing or ask students to complete different components of a writing process and expect that they will become independent, skilled writers. Louise Clark made the following observation:

I sat down with Mike and made a jolting discovery. *He knew what he had written.* Furthermore, with him to do the decoding, the answers were correct. I remember "Nloond" particularly. It was in answer to a question on the third line down over to the right of the page, "London," Mike said impatiently (1974).

GRADUAL RELEASE OF RESPONSIBILITY WRITING INSTRUCTIONAL FRAMEWORK

WRITING INSTRUCTIONAL APPROACH	PURPOSE	LEVEL OF TEACHER SUPPORT
Language Experience Approach	Make connections between speech and print.	**Extensive** Teacher models layout of a short written message and applies conventions of print.
Interactive Writing	Compose collaborative written messages based on group discussion.	**Significant** Teacher scaffolds conversion of students' oral composition to written message.
Power Writing	Build writing fluency.	**Moderate** Teacher prompts and encourages students' sustained writing for a short, timed period.
Generative Writing	Work with word, sentence, and paragraph boundaries in order to refine word choice, grammar, and sentence construction.	**Modest** Teacher gives students specific criteria for writing syntactic and semantic features in an original text.
Writing Models	Study and apply the techniques other writers use.	**Limited** Teacher provides a frame to scaffold students' writing for a longer piece.
Independent Writing Prompts	Create original texts that are purposeful, well-crafted, and accurate.	**Minimal** Teacher assists students as needed.

Most students, like Mike, write the best they can each time they write. However, in the absence of instruction and feedback, their writing looks fine to them. Our concern is that in too many classrooms the emphasis is on independent writing at the expense of writing instruction. With appropriate instruction, students are able to acquire new skills and practice them at the elbows of others until they are able to perform the tasks independently. This is achieved through a workshop model of instruction.

The Workshop Model

The writing workshop is built on a gradual-release framework, going from focus lessons to guided instruction to collaborative learning and, finally, to independent writing. Each component of the workshop is intended to move

WRITING WORKSHOP MODEL

WRITING WORKSHOP INSTRUCTIONAL FORMAT	PURPOSE	LEVEL OF TEACHER SUPPORT
Focus Lesson (whole class)	Learn or review a writing skill or strategy.	**Extensive** Teacher models and demonstrates the skill or strategy through a teacher-directed lesson.
Guided Instruction (small groups— up to 6 students)	Apply a newly learned skill or strategy with teacher assistance.	**Significant** Teacher assists individual students with difficulties in applying the target skill/strategy.
Collaborative Learning (pairs or small groups)	Apply a newly learned skill or strategy with peers.	**Moderate** Teacher coordinates peer groups and sets parameters for the assignment.
Independent Writing (individual)	Independently create original texts by consolidating new and previously learned skills and strategies.	**Minimal** Teacher assists students as needed.

students from watching a knowledgeable other perform a task to independently implementing that task. The figure on page 13 presents an overview of the components of the workshop.

In the introduction, you met Ms. Aida Allen and her student, Tino. As we discuss the different components of the workshop, we'll present brief examples from her class. But first, here's some background on Ms. Allen and her class.

Ms. Allen is an experienced fifth-grade teacher from Rosa Parks Elementary School in San Diego, California. In addition to Tino, there are thirty-two other students in her class. All the students are bilingual, speaking Spanish and English, and all qualify for free lunch. Of these thirty-three students, three receive special education services. The students range from newcomers who have recently arrived from Mexico to longtime residents. The reading skills in this class range from first to twelfth grade according to the Stanford Diagnostic Reading Test. The average for the class is 4.1, which is about a year below grade level.

→ FOCUS LESSON

During a focus lesson, the teacher models and demonstrates a writing skill or strategy while students observe. As the focus lesson progresses, the teacher begins to create opportunities for students to try the skill or strategy themselves.

PREVIEW: Early in the year, Ms. Allen teaches a focus lesson on writing fluency. Her objective in this first lesson is to teach a procedure called Power Writing, which she will use as a daily writing exercise for the rest of the school year. During each Power Writing session, students will engage in a series of one-minute drills to increase their ability to get ideas down on paper. Ms. Allen knows that writing fluency is an important quality that all good writers possess. However, she must first get her students comfortable with Power Writing.

After explaining the purpose and procedure for timed writing drills, Ms. Allen models how it is done. She uses a think-aloud approach as she writes continuously for one minute. During this timed writing, Ms. Allen models what she is thinking. At the beginning of her paragraph, she stalls briefly and says, "I'm stuck on a word, but I'm going to keep going. Right now my goal is to write as much as I can, as well as I can."

As she writes on the overhead projector, Ms. Allen tells the class what she is thinking. Her paragraph and think-aloud appear below.

PARAGRAPH AND THINK-ALOUD

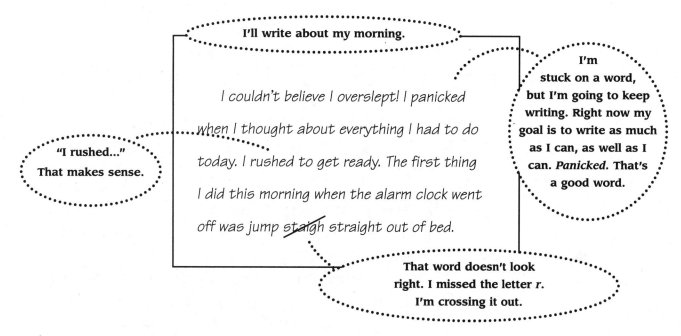

After observing and discussing, the students do a timed writing of one minute. Ms. Allen coaches her young writers as they write.

→ GUIDED INSTRUCTION

Guided instruction is designed to offer specific lessons for small groups of learners. Every student in the class is selected for a guided instruction group based on the assessment data the teacher has collected. The focus of the instruction differs for each group, however, since it's based on the needs of the students in each group. As the teacher assesses students' progress, they can move among groups.

Because the guided instruction group consists of six or fewer students, a teacher can offer higher levels of support than in a whole-group situation. However, guided instruction is not just more intensive modeling. The lesson begins with a review of the skill or strategy introduced in the focus lesson. Then there is a quick shift in responsibility as the learner uses the new skill or strategy in an original way.

PREVIEW: Ms. Allen introduces the use of a fluency exercise in the previous focus lesson. She then selects a small group of students who need additional guided practice. Ms. Allen begins by saying:

"You've seen me do a timed writing and you've had a chance to try it for yourselves. Now we're going to get better at it by doing a cycle of three one-minute writings. After you've finished, we'll count words and circle any mistakes. Remember our motto: Write as much as you can, as well as you can. I'll give you a word to jump-start your thinking. I'd like for you to use the word *pony* in your writing. Ready? Pencils up!" She sets the timer for one minute. "Begin!"

For the next minute, the six students in the group write furiously. When Robert pauses, Ms. Allen says, "Keep going. You can even write the same word again until you're ready for the next idea."

When Miriam lifts her pencil and looks puzzled at the word she has just written, Ms. Allen says, "Does that word look funny to you? That happens to me, too, when I'm writing fast. If you can't fix it right away, circle it and come back to it later."

As the timer rings, she asks the students to reread what they have written, circling errors in spelling or grammar. Then she tells them to count their words and write the number in the margin of their paper.

The group repeats this routine three times. Each time, Ms. Allen assists any students who are stuck. She discusses the errors they notice and makes note of those that have escaped their attention. The small-group work enables students having trouble to practice new fluency strategies and receive support and feedback right away.

→ COLLABORATIVE LEARNING

During the collaborative learning phase of the workshop, students work in pairs or small groups to write. The teacher is not present as he or she was in the guided instruction groups. This is perhaps the most critical portion of the workshop because now students will use the language of writers to make meaning. The emphasis here is not just on being a writer; it is also on using oral language to explain, negotiate, clarify, and question one another during a shared experience. Students must alternate between being the speaker and the listener as they consider the requirements of the task as well as the input of another person. As Pauline Gibbons writes:

> If children are to "learn by talking," then we must also create classroom situations where they have opportunities to be confronted by viewpoints not necessarily their own and discuss possible solutions to a problem with their peers. . . . In a whole class discussion it is likely that the teacher will take responsibility for holding the discussion together . . . [i]n a two-person dialogue there is far more opportunity for both speakers to engage in a piece of connected and cohesive discourse (1991).

Of course, as writing teachers, our ears perk up at the notion of "connected and cohesive discourse," for this is at the heart of good writing. By ensuring that students have frequent collaborative writing experiences, we increase the likelihood that they have something to write about. In essence, the collaborative learning event becomes oral composition as each writer prepares a piece of text. At times, the writers try ideas on for size by telling a peer what they are thinking about for their writing. On other occasions, the young writers may be working on a piece together.

PREVIEW: The class has been Power Writing for two weeks. Ms. Allen wants students to look at their writing samples to consider expanding some into a more polished piece. Coraima and Mariana work together to choose writing samples. With their Power Writing journals opened, the girls read the task card Ms. Allen has placed at the writing station (see page 18).

Coraima begins by reading a Power Writing sample from the previous day. "I went to see my cousin get baptized last weekend. My aunts and uncles were there. My cousin is cute. His name is Gabriel."

Mariana then asks questions about the sample. "Did that really happen?"

"Yes, on Saturday. We went to the church first, then to my tia Maria's for

```
COLLABORATIVE WRITING TASK CARD #3
```

Your task today:

Read some of your Power Writing samples to one another and select at least one to expand into a longer piece.

How to:

Step 1: Read your Power Writing samples to your partner.

Step 2: Listen as your writing partner comments on your samples. Look for ideas that are interesting, funny, or surprising.

Step 3: With the help of your partner, choose one Power Writing sample that you are going to turn into a more polished piece. This can include:
   • autobiographical incident   • report of information
   • poem   • short story   • song lyrics

Step 4: Repeat Steps 1–3 with your partner's writing.

---

the party," replies Coraima.

Mariana probes for details. "Was it fun? Did anything funny happen?"

Coraima appears to think for a moment, then tells her writing partner that it was sometimes boring, but the funniest part was when the baby cried so loud during the ceremony that no one could hear.

"You could write about that," offers Mariana. "You'd have to tell more about it, but you could use it when you need an idea to write about."

Coraima puts a star next to this sample and writes, "Tell about the baby crying" in the margin. This may later become a piece in her writer's journal.

→ INDEPENDENT WRITING

This final component in the writing workshop signals the moment we are all working toward: when a student freely applies a skill or strategy correctly. Our concern lies only with skipping the other components of the workshop in a rush to move directly to independent writing. Working with all the workshop components ensures that a young writer is ready to apply the skill or strategy because it has become a part of his or her repertoire.

PREVIEW: Ms. Allen has asked her students to expand a Power Writing sample into a longer piece. "Let's keep this short," she announces. "I'd like for you to think about your conversation with your writing partner. Turn this into a short piece—no more than 100 words." As students begin to write, Ms. Allen speaks quietly with individual students, offering support for spelling and word choice. During their independent work, students select and refine ideas they've developed during Power Writing and apply composition skills they've learned. Ms. Allen uses these pieces to evaluate their progress and pinpoint areas for reteaching.

The Big Seven Approaches: An Instructional Framework

Because the instructional approaches included in our framework (page 12) are so adaptable, their usefulness is not limited to a particular age or skill level. Teachers of students with different needs and different readiness levels adjust their instruction using writing workshop components to provide the appropriate support (page 13).

Let's preview each of the instructional approaches used in this framework once again through the lens of Ms. Allen's classroom. Notice how in every scenario, Ms. Allen aims to shift responsibility for composing the message increasingly into the hands of the students. (Although we focus on Ms. Allen and her fifth graders in this chapter, you'll find examples from many other grade levels and teachers in the chapters that follow.)

→ LANGUAGE EXPERIENCE APPROACH (LEA)

LEA is an instructional approach first developed in 1963 by Sylvia Ashton-Warner to meet the needs of young students just learning to read and write. Using LEA, a teacher solicits language from a student about an experience. As the child speaks, the teacher takes dictation. The goal of LEA is to help children connect their speech with printed text—a critical stage in the development of literacy users. The written text becomes material the teacher can use in reading instruction because the child is familiar with every word as well as the content of the message. Students are able to concentrate on the content of his or her message and the syntax of the sentences since they are freed from having to write the message independently.

Although LEA is utilized to develop speech-to-print connections, its usefulness is not limited to generating reading material for beginning readers. In this framework, the language experience approach is also used to model writing, often in a group setting. As the teacher and students create the message, the teacher writes the words for everyone to see. These sentences are about a shared experience or a topic of study. They serve as a starter for further writing by individual students. After copying the message into their journals, students write additional information.

PREVIEW: Ms. Allen uses LEA to record her class's response to a field trip to a local museum. As her students discuss the trip, she shapes the message to craft the written text. She asks questions about word choice and the content of the message. For example, students discuss the use of the words *weird* and *odd* in describing their reaction to the field trip. After a brief debate on the merits of each word, the class agrees that *odd* is the best choice. The message the students compose with Ms. Allen reads:

> *Our trip to the Museum of Man was awesome! One of our favorite experiences was making the mummified apples. We also saw shrunken heads. They were odd looking.*

Later, Ms. Allen has her students extend the message by writing two or three more sentences about their individual recommendations to others who visit the museum.

The role of the teacher in LEA is to model writing through the transcription process while students participate in developing the message. In addition, students observe as the teacher writes their message on the board or page. Because LEA composition cannot occur without the teacher, this approach demands extensive teacher support. While traditional LEA has been done with one student at a time, we use this process in small and large groups, as well as with individual learners. We have found that the most important aspect of LEA is allowing time for discussion to develop so that the final message reflects understanding among all participants.

→ INTERACTIVE WRITING

Interactive writing has emerged as an outgrowth of the language experience approach. As with LEA, interactive writing offers students an opportunity to engage in oral composition before their message is written. However, a hallmark of interactive writing instruction is in who holds the pen. While the teacher is the writer in LEA, students take turns writing portions of the message with guidance from the teacher in interactive writing lessons.

A typical lesson begins with a discussion of the purpose for the writing and the audience. The teacher facilitates a conversation about the exact wording of the message and then moves to composing it on chart paper (or the board). Students take turns writing individual letters or words on the chart paper to complete the message while the teacher scaffolds their understanding. He or she uses questions and prompts that invite students to solve problems that may include letter formation, spelling, or layout on the page. Throughout the interactive writing lesson, the entire message is repeated after each word. If the message is lengthy, it may take more than one session to complete.

PREVIEW: In this lesson, Ms. Allen uses inter-active writing instruction to create a formal thank-you letter to a guest speaker. She begins by establishing the purpose and audience and assists the class in determining the wording and format of the letter. Ms. Allen and her students discuss the layout of a friendly letter, including indenta-tions and conventions about a salutation before writing. Then individual students write the words from the message they are familiar with on the chart paper, completing the message as a group.

At times, with students learning English, Ms. Allen works at the individual letter level. For example, when it is Alejandra's turn, she strug-gles with the spelling of the word *beginning*. Knowing that students who speak Spanish as a first language often have trouble with double consonants, Ms. Allen asks her to say the word aloud and listen for the accented syllable. "Be-GIN-ing, be-GIN-ing," Alejandra says slowly.

"When there's an accent on the second syllable, what happens?" asks Ms. Allen.

"Double it up!" smiles Alejandra, recalling the spelling rule.

An important feature of interactive writing instruction is the student's role in writing individual letters and words. Yet the teacher continues to play a significant role in the process because of the high levels of scaffold-ing that occur throughout the lesson. The teacher also corrects errors immediately, usually with white tape so the final product is accurate. Because the writing is done on a large chart, all the students can see how the message develops on the page.

Interactive writing represents a deceptively simple form of instruction because the scaffolding required demands that the teacher understand the processes writers use to plan, compose, and monitor a message. In addition, the teacher must be aware of the current knowledge level of his or her students in order to solicit correct solutions to the "tricky parts" encountered along the way.

→ POWER WRITING

Earlier in this chapter we introduced Power Writing through the writing workshop model in examples from Ms. Allen's classroom. Power Writing is a daily fluency-building technique that consists of brief, timed writing events. During Power Writing sessions students are instructed to write as much as they can as well as they can about a topic. These one-minute writing intervals are performed up to three times in a row.

An important part of the gradual-release framework, writing fluency instruction supports the research on writing sentence parts. In the introduction, we discussed how expert writers construct longer strings of sentence parts before pausing than less skilled writers do. Writing fluency exercises encourage writers to get their thoughts down on paper quickly and increasingly fluidly—and not to procrastinate or start and stop as many of us do when faced with a writing task.

The format for Power Writing is easy to implement in the classroom. The teacher reminds students about the purpose of the exercise (to write as much as they can as well they can), presents a topic, and then offers a word to be used somewhere in their writing. He or she sets a timer for one minute, and students begin to write. After the timer rings, students reread their writing. They circle any words they believe they've spelled or used incorrectly. Students also record the number of words they wrote in the margin. The same procedure is completed two more times. Each time, the teacher uses a different word or phrase.

After the third cycle, each student records his or her best result on a graph that is kept in a writer's notebook. Nearly all the students will discover they wrote more words the third time than they did on the first attempt, which is a sure sign that they are building fluency. The graph serves as an incentive for students and allows them to gauge their growing proficiency as fluent writers. Occasionally, the teacher has students select a Power Writing passage as a starter for an expanded piece of writing.

PREVIEW: Ms. Allen begins each morning with a Power Writing session. Since she has been working with her class on writing compare/contrast paragraphs, she wants to gauge the effectiveness of her instruction. Ms. Allen selects words that are transitional devices for comparative statements to use in this Power Writing session.

She writes the word *Meanwhile* on the board. Before setting the timer for one minute, she gives the following instructions to students: "Write as much as you can, as well as you can for one minute. Begin your writing with the word *Meanwhile*."

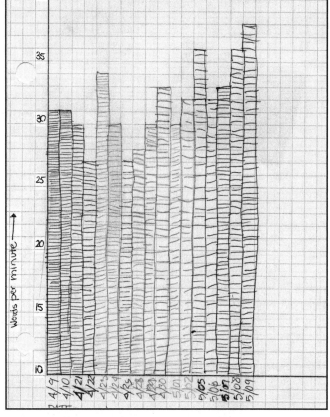

The students write for one minute. After the timer rings, they reread their writing and circle errors. Then they count the total number of words. For the second and third sessions, Ms. Allen chooses the words *However* and *Yet*. When students finish with their corrections and word counts, they record their highest number of words in their graphs.

Because the responsibility for composing the message now rests on the student, Power Writing represents a further shift in the level of teacher support. While the teacher supplies the prompts to facilitate writing, it is the student who must construct meaningful text and sustain it across a brief passage. The teacher's role is also to manage the session and to tell students when to begin writing and when to stop.

→ GENERATIVE WRITING

Generative writing instruction is designed to promote a consolidation of the syntactic (grammar) and semantic (meaning) knowledge of the writer in developing individual sentences. Like Power Writing, the teacher provides a prompt to serve as the criteria for the sentence. This prompt may consist of a word accompanied by a directive about the relative position of the word within the sentence. (For example, the instruction "Place the word *civic* in the second position" might elicit the sentence "A civic holiday, Memorial Day is a day to recognize and remember the service and sacrifice of our armed forces.") And, like Power Writing, generative writing instruction is typically brief—usually ten minutes or so.

PREVIEW: Ms. Allen's class is studying plate tectonics in science. She asks students to use the word *volcanoes* in the fourth position in a sentence.

"We've been studying how sections of the earth called plates move. The movement of these plates can cause earthquakes and volcanic eruptions. Today, I'd like you to write a sentence that has the word *volcano* in the fourth position. You'll have two minutes to think of a sentence and write it down."

Different students write the following sentences:

Scientists who study <u>volcanoes</u> are called volcanologists.

The name for <u>volcanoes</u> in the Pacific is the "Ring of Fire."

I don't like <u>volcanoes</u>.

Families fled the <u>volcanoes</u> molten lava.

While the first three sentences are correct, they reflect a range of understanding about the knowledge level of each writer. The fourth sentence contains an error in its syntactic structure: instead of using the possessive form of the word, this student substituted the plural form. By responding constructively to unsuccessful attempts to use a word in a sentence, you can help increase students' vocabulary and sentence construction skills.

Variations in generative writing instruction exist, such as having students use the same word in a series of positions or offering a prompt that begins at the letter level first. For instance, teachers of younger students may begin by asking for a word that begins with the letter "g". Students may variously write words such as *give, giant*, and *giraffes.* Next, they are told to use the word in the first position, resulting in sentences like this:

<u>Give</u> me that book.

<u>Giant</u> otters live in the Amazon.

<u>Giraffes</u> are at the zoo.

Generative writing lessons begin with instruction around the focus of the sentence and then move to brief independent writing using the generative sentence as a starting point. You can vary the degree of support you offer as well as the complexity of the sentence construction task. The teacher's role is generally more modest as students assume more control of the writing while they consider the syntactic and semantic features of their sentences.

→ WRITING MODELS

Writing models serve as a framework for students to use to create sustained written pieces. A writing model consists of a pattern or an excerpt of a previously published work around which students create original writing. It's more than just a fill-in-the-blank approach because the overall text must present a unified set of ideas.

A simple example of a patterned writing frame is *haiku*, a traditional form of Japanese poetry. The poem is a seventeen-syllable verse arranged in three lines consisting of five, seven, and five syllables each. Another type of writing model uses a frame from published work that can be adapted for student-generated writing.

PREVIEW: The picture book *It's Okay to Be Different* by Todd Parr uses the repetitive frame "It's okay to..." at the beginning of each sentence. After reading and discussing the book and its meaning, Ms. Allen invites her students to use this writing model to write an original version of the book: "Now we're going to write our own book called *It's Okay*. I'd like each of you to write a sentence that begins with these words: *It's okay to...*" The students write the following sentences:

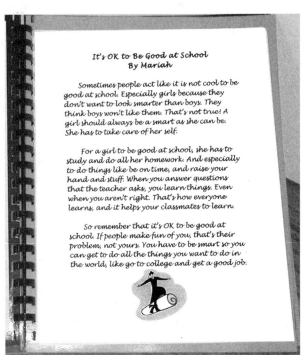

It's okay to do good at school.

It's okay to stand up for what's right.

It's okay to feel afraid sometimes.

Ms. Allen asks them to share their sentences and create a page for the class book with the one they've chosen. Entitled *It's Okay to Be a Fifth Grader*, this book quickly becomes a class favorite and students begin to use the format in their independent writing. Later the *It's okay...*

sentences will become the titles and springboards for short essays written by students on the challenges of growing up.

When a teacher applies a writing model in the classroom, the level of support he or she offers is generally limited to introducing the concept. Students assume more control of the writing as they seek to develop and sustain the concept across a longer piece of text.

→ INDEPENDENT WRITING

Independent writing is both the most independent of all the approaches introduced in the framework as well as the goal of writing instruction, for ultimately we strive for all students to be able to write well and purposefully on their own. Unlike many other academic skills, the ability to write independently cannot be viewed as something that stands apart from other cognitive processes such as reading, oral language, and content knowledge. Indeed, as Anne Dyson and Sarah Freedman suggest, "written language is always 'embedded'; it always figures into particular kinds of communicative events. Its form varies depending on its uses" (2003).

Nor can independent writing be viewed as something to be "earned" only after sufficient achievement is attained in other writing processes or strategies. As we have stated before, the gradual-release framework is not a hierarchy of skills; rather, it is an approach to systematically instruct students about the many aspects of effective writing. Therefore, independent writing should occur daily beginning on the first day of kindergarten and continuing throughout a student's academic career. However, let us remind you that the exclusive use of independent writing will *not* result in students who write more and better. Other approaches and strategies must be used simultaneously and these must be chosen based on the specific needs of the learners you teach—as groups and individuals in the class.

Independent writing can occur in many forms. For instance, daily journal writing gives students the time and space to write about the things that interest them. You may also have students engage in brief "writing to learn" events to clarify their understanding about a topic or concept or respond to specific prompts, with an understanding of the rubric that will be used to assess their writing.

PREVIEW: While her class is studying plate tectonics, Ms. Allen asks her students to expand the generative sentences they have written about volcanoes for an independent writing practice. (See page 24.)

> The name for volcanoes in the Pacific is called the Ring of Fire. These are the volcanoes in Hawii, South America, and Asia. Some are active. That means they erupt. Some are dormant. That means they are quiet.

Reports, essays, poems, instructions, lists, and e-mails represent just a smattering of the forms of independent writing that students can use. Some independent writing events are initiated by a prompt that assigns a task and a purpose for the writing. Many of these prompts have been influenced in the last decade by the rise in state- and district-mandated writing assessments. Although the specifics of what is assessed and when it is assessed vary by state, these writing-on-demand assessments typically focus on common formats for writing including the following:

- *biographical and autobiographical narratives*
- *summary writing*
- *response to literature*
- *persuasive essays*
- *informative writing*

The amount of support the teacher offers during independent writing decreases as students truly consolidate their knowledge of the skills and strategies they currently know to produce meaningful text that conforms to grade-level expectations. The teacher is available to consult and coach as needed, but the writing itself is under the command of the writer.

In Chapters 3–8, we explain each of these approaches in detail, helping you to put the ideas into practice. But first, let's discuss the integral part that assessment plays in the gradual release of responsibility framework. Chapter 2 provides tools that help you monitor students' progress and plan for instruction.

Writing Assessments and Feedback

Now that you understand why purposeful writing instruction is so important, it's time to begin planning. Noticing differences in student writing performance is critical for making your instruction effective. As teachers, we understand the importance of using assessment data to inform our instruction. We think of it as a way to get closer to a target. Not utilizing assessment information is akin to standing far away from your target—the likelihood of hitting a bulls-eye is greatly reduced. Armed with assessment information, we move closer to the target, increasing our chances of offering the right instruction at the right time.

As Diane Lapp and James Flood (2003) note, "Because of the range of literacy skills that will exist among students at any grade, it is very important that teachers continuously observe and assess student performance, identify strengths, diagnose needs, and plan instruction." In other words, assessment information guides our instruction and ensures that we are meeting the individual needs of students. There is ample evidence to indicate that planning instruction based on assessment information is important for student achievement. On the surface, this seems logical and simple. In reality, it is complex and involved.

That "range of literacy skills" that Lapp and Flood noted exists *within* students as well. In our own teaching, we have been confused at times with the performance of individual students when it comes to writing. Among our hardest-to-teach students, there exists a unique blend of strengths and needs. In fact, we believe that good writers often have much in common with each other, while struggling writers tend to be unlike fellow strugglers.

This chapter provides information on the development of young writers, the writing assessments that should be routinely conducted, and some data collection and recordkeeping tools that may be useful in storing assessment information. It concludes with a discussion of the ways in which students can be involved in assessment, specifically regarding the type of feedback they will find helpful as they become proficient writers. We begin with an assessment portrait of a student and his teacher. We chose the following vignette as a reminder that writing assessment encompasses more than the student's writing. It is one element of a learner's literacy portrait, and therefore, his or her oral and reading assessments should be viewed as a lens to his writing.

Reaching E. J.: Portrait of a Struggling Writer

Ms. Abrams had a student in fourth grade named E. J., who could spin imaginative tales about his exploits and adventures. (He once entertained the entire class with a retelling of *Charlie and the Chocolate Factory* that placed him and several of his classmates at the center of the story.) Yet when it came time to write, E. J. seemed to freeze. The spoken language that flowed so easily when he had an audience seemed to dry up when confronted with a blank page. The little that E. J. wrote was flat, formulaic at best, and utterly devoid of his lively personality.

An examination of E. J.'s written work would have revealed only one dimension of his academic needs and strengths. Ms. Abrams had introduced an attribute writing rubric to the class at the beginning of the year, based on elements of good writing: content, organization, word choice, details, and conventions (see page 30). E. J.'s early writing scored low on this rubric. Here is the opening paragraph of a paper he wrote in September as a response to the question, "What do you like to do on a rainy day?"

> *I like to watch the simpsons on TV. My brother favorite cartoon is the simpsons. I like how the simpson make there cartoon.*

The rubric score suggested that E. J. was a poor writer and further pointed out that he had particular difficulty with content, word choices, and conventions. However, this single assessment missed the other things that Ms. Abrams already knew about E. J.—he possessed a vivid imagination (we might call this *content*), a sly sense of humor (we might call this *details* and *word choice*), and a sense of what his audience needed to make his tales understandable (we might call this *organization* and *conventions*).

Content, details, word choice, organization, conventions—do they sound familiar? They are the same elements Ms. Abrams used on her rubric.

CLASSROOM ATTRIBUTE WRITING RUBRIC FROM FOURTH GRADE

Writing Element	3	2	1
Content	The topic is clearly stated.	There is a topic, but it is not stated.	It is hard to find the topic.
Organization	There is an order to the ideas that helps the reader to understand.	It is sometimes hard for the reader to follow the ideas.	The ideas are confusing to the reader because ideas are skipped or out of order.
Word Choice	The author uses interesting words accurately and to make the writing lively.	Some simpler words are overused (*like*, *said*, *nice*).	The author doesn't use a variety of words, or uses them incorrectly.
Details	The author uses details that make the writing interesting and understandable.	There are details, although some may be unnecessary or in the wrong place.	The author left out details that make the writing interesting and understandable.
Conventions	Good first draft, with few or no spelling and grammar errors.	The spelling or grammar errors are sometimes distracting.	The spelling or grammar errors make it hard for the reader to understand the writing.

E. J. had a sense of all these elements. He just needed to learn how to use them in his writing. If Ms. Abrams had restricted her writing assessments to his *written* work alone, she would have missed this.

But Ms. Abrams looked again at the reading assessment information she had collected on E. J. He was reading at grade level, as determined by an informal reading inventory used by her school district. Measures of reading comprehension, determined by answering literal and inferential questions, also appeared on level. Scoring as a late within-word-pattern speller, his developmental spelling inventory was lower than expected for a fourth grader. However, E. J.'s oral language was a real strength. Ms. Abrams had used an oral language checklist to gauge his performance in several settings, including peer talk, academic discussions, and social situations. He excelled at retellings, listened closely in conversations, and was adept in social conversations. Overall, these assessments revealed a student who

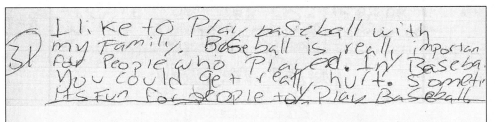

Text: *I like to play baseball with my family. Baseball is really important for people who played. In baseball you could get really hurt. Sometimes its fun for people to play baseball.*

E. J.'s journal entry showed that he had little sentence fluency and used limited word choices.

read well, understood what he read, and used oral language to his advantage both academically and socially. An area of concern was his spelling, which was comparatively lower than his other literacy processes.

Ms. Abrams then returned to the task of evaluating E. J.'s written work. She used her state's fourth-grade writing rubric as a foundation and examined three representational pieces: a ten-minute timed writing exercise, a journal entry from his writer's notebook, and a social studies report on the United Kingdom he had written.

Ms. Abrams noted that E. J. struggled with organization and sentence fluency, as evidenced by the choppy and stilted flow of ideas in his journal entry. Yet when she spoke to him, he was full of information and seemed eager to share his ideas with an audience. His attention to conventions, especially capitalization and punctuation, was fitful, and she noticed that it seemed to vary depending on the amount of time he had and his level of interest. It seemed that E. J. possessed both strengths and needs as a writer.

Ms. Abrams concluded her assessment with an interview designed to reveal E. J.'s attitude toward writing. The Writing Attitude Survey (Kear, Coffman, McKenna, & Ambrosio, 2000) is a normed instrument containing 28 items such as, "How would you feel if you could write more in school?" and "How would you feel if your classmates talked to you about making your writing better?" E. J. scored a 72 out of a possible 112 points, placing him at the 32nd percentile among fourth graders. His answers provided insight into his perceptions of himself as a writer. E. J. possessed a strong interest in science and social studies topics, but he didn't like revising and making corrections. In particular, he saw writing as the least preferred choice among alternatives such as watching television or even doing homework.

→ TEACHING E. J.:
MOVING FROM ASSESSMENT TO INSTRUCTION

Based on the reading, writing, and oral language assessments she had gathered, Ms. Abrams determined that E. J. would benefit from a developmental writing approach based on a gradual release of responsibility framework. In particular, she felt that E. J. would profit from lots of experience with Language Experience Approach (LEA) to show him how to get his ideas down on paper. In addition, she would use interactive writing with E. J. and a small group of peers so that they could focus on the conventions of writing. Ms. Abrams felt that he knew many of these rules in theory, but he got bogged down in the decisions needed at the point of use.

E. J.'s use of ideas and conventions converged in fluency instruction. Ms. Abrams used daily timed writing events (Power Writing) with the entire class to increase students' ability to commit words to paper more rapidly. Because E. J.'s writing attitudes revealed an unmotivated writer, she made sure to confer weekly with him on his progress with Power Writing. The anecdotal notes Ms. Abrams kept of these conferences mentioned E. J.'s growing pride as his average words per minute increased.

Generative sentences were an important part of E. J.'s instruction as well. In particular, Ms. Abrams emphasized word choice with her students. They developed skills at using the thesaurus and worked with one another during the peer feedback process to ask each other questions about word choice in their writing. All of her students practiced using complex and compound sentences to make their writing more interesting. E. J.'s strengths in oral language served him well; he often composed his ideas verbally with peers before writing to develop more sophisticated sentences.

E. J. received instruction throughout the year in using writing models and frames to develop original writing. Ms. Abrams modeled sentence fluency, especially in demonstrating how transition words and phrases are used. E. J. needed quite a bit of assistance at writing paragraphs that "hung together" to meet the needs of his readers. Throughout the year, Ms. Abrams and her class wrote many types of paragraphs, including explanatory, descriptive, persuasive, and comparison and contrast.

They evaluated the paragraphs they created together and independently by using a series of checklists designed for each type of writing. Ms. Abrams modeled the use of these checklists in her focus lessons, and students used the checklists collaboratively as they read and commented on each other's work. (Sample checklists for different types of paragraphs appear on pages 33–34.)

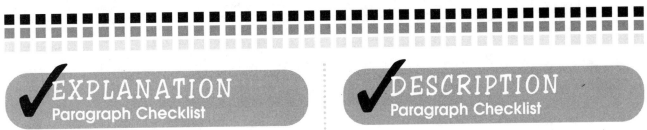

✔ EXPLANATION
Paragraph Checklist

Name of writer: _____

Name of reader: _____

Title or topic: _____

_____

Explanation and How-to Paragraphs

❑ Does the reader know what your paragraph is explaining?

❑ Is the information correct?

❑ Are all the important steps or facts included?

❑ Can a reader repeat your directions?

❑ Are the sentences written clearly?

❑ Are the sentences written accurately? (spelling, punctuation, grammar)

Ideas for making it better:

_____

_____

_____

_____

_____

_____

_____

_____

✔ DESCRIPTION
Paragraph Checklist

Name of writer: _____

Name of reader: _____

Title or topic: _____

_____

Description Paragraphs

❑ Does the reader know what is being described?

❑ Does the author compare it to something else?

❑ Is the description accurate?

❑ Does the author use descriptive words?

❑ Are the sentences written clearly?

❑ Are the sentences written accurately? (spelling, punctuation, grammar)

Ideas for making it better:

_____

_____

_____

_____

_____

_____

_____

_____

✔ PERSUASIVE
Paragraph Checklist

Name of writer: _____

Name of reader: _____

Title or topic: _____

_____

Persuasive Paragraphs

❑ Does the reader know the author's opinion?

❑ Does the reader know why the author holds this opinion? (Look for words like *because*.)

❑ Is it accurate?

❑ Does the author use strong words to persuade?

❑ Are the sentences written clearly?

❑ Are the sentences written accurately? (spelling, punctuation, grammar)

Ideas for making it better:

_____

_____

_____

_____

_____

_____

_____

_____

✔ COMPARE/CONTRAST
Paragraph Checklist

Name of writer: _____

Name of reader: _____

Title or topic: _____

_____

Comparing or Contrasting Paragraphs

❑ Does the reader know the two things that are being compared or contrasted?

❑ Does the author explain how they are alike or different?

❑ Is the information accurate?

❑ Are the sentences written clearly?

❑ Are the sentences written accurately? (spelling, punctuation, grammar)

Ideas for making it better:

_____

_____

_____

_____

_____

_____

_____

_____

Ms. Abrams periodically assessed timed writing samples from E. J. and others using the following parameters:

- *total number of words written*

- *total number of sentences written*

- *average length of sentences (divide total number of words by total number of sentences)*

- *average number of convention errors per sentence*

This allowed her to monitor his writing fluency and use of more complex sentences in his writing.

Ms. Abrams' writing program also included daily independent writing. E. J. and her other students wrote many short pieces because she wanted all of them to complete their writing without bogging down in processes that reduce the overall output of students. E. J. seemed especially sensitive to this, and responded positively to assignments that allowed him to create short, manageable pieces. Ms. Abrams also asked her students to review their writer's notebooks each week for ideas to expand into longer pieces. She established peer response time so that young writers could get a reader's take on their writing. E. J. reacted positively to this, confirming what she had discovered about him during the writing attitude survey—he preferred working with peers.

→ E. J. SEES HIMSELF AS A WRITER

E. J. progressed as a writer throughout his fourth-grade year. Ms. Abrams used a variety of assessments to monitor his progress, including the following:

- *holistic rubrics*

- *fluency graphs for Power Writing*

- *timed writings to assess the number of words and sentences, as well as average sentence length*

- *checklists for types of writing*

- *anecdotal notes collected at writing conferences*

- *peer response conferences*

- *attitude surveys*

- *reading and oral language measures*

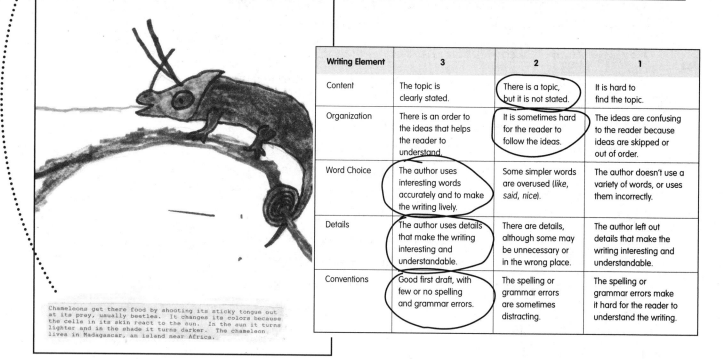

Chameleons get there food by shooting its sticky tongue out at its prey, usually beetles. It changes its colors because the cells in its skin react to the sun. In the sun it turns lighter and in the shade it turns darker. The chameleon lives in Madagascar, an island near Africa.

Writing Element	3	2	1
Content	The topic is clearly stated.	There is a topic, but it is not stated.	It is hard to find the topic.
Organization	There is an order to the ideas that helps the reader to understand.	It is sometimes hard for the reader to follow the ideas.	The ideas are confusing to the reader because ideas are skipped or out of order.
Word Choice	The author uses interesting words accurately and to make the writing lively.	Some simpler words are overused (like, said, nice).	The author doesn't use a variety of words, or uses them incorrectly.
Details	The author uses details that make the writing interesting and understandable.	There are details, although some may be unnecessary or in the wrong place.	The author left out details that make the writing interesting and understandable.
Conventions	Good first draft, with few or no spelling and grammar errors.	The spelling or grammar errors are sometimes distracting.	The spelling or grammar errors make it hard for the reader to understand the writing.

Within a few months, E. J. was increasingly using writing as a vehicle for self-expression. In the spring of his fourth-grade year, he wrote a handbook on chameleons (a favorite subject) and published it on the classroom computer, accompanied by his own drawings.

Text: *Chameleons get there food by shooting its sticky tongue out at its prey, usually beetles. It changes its colors because the cells in its skin react to the sun. In the sun it turns lighter and in shade it turns darker. The chameleon lives in Madagascar, an island near Africa.*

What a difference in E. J.'s writing! Using Ms. Abram's holistic writing rubric from page 30, E. J. is shown to be a writer with good control of content, organization, word choice, details, and conventions. He earns a score of 13 (out of 15), as shown above.

Assessing Writing: Understanding the Writer's Development

Assessment information allows us to identify the type of instruction students need. These instructional decisions are balanced by our understanding of the developmental progression of young writers. We do know that students progress through phases as they learn to write—emerging, early, transitional, and newly fluent. From the information provided about each type of writer, teachers can get a sense of the instructional needs their students have.

EMERGING WRITERS. Children new to writing (and reading) will exhibit a number of behaviors that are recognizable as indicators of this phase. These writers may use nontraditional means for recording their messages, including scribbling, drawing, and letters that may represent the sounds of the words. Emerging writers are beginning to understand that there is a 1:1 correspondence between the spoken and written word. Most importantly, they know that print carries a message that can be interpreted and understood by others. Although this book does not focus on emerging writers, it is important to understand where our young writers have been.

EARLY WRITERS. Students in this phase of writing development have greater control over their spelling and are beginning to use multiple sentences to explain and describe. However, these sentences are simply constructed and do not have much of a flow (sentence fluency). Students use primary dictionaries to check for words and their stories are constructed using basic story grammar, especially a beginning and ending. The progression from beginning to end may not be completely logical.

TRANSITIONAL WRITERS. This is an exciting phase of development in the lives of young writers and their teachers. Transitional writers are experimenting with genres and writing longer, multi-paragraph pieces. They use conventions, compound sentences, and word choice more proficiently. Transitional writers are beginning to understand the usefulness of information from outside sources in their own original writing. E. J.'s writing samples show him progressing from an early to a transitional writer.

NEWLY FLUENT WRITERS. These writers show a level of maturity and flexibility in their writing. They select genres to meet their own needs and acknowledge the role of the audience in their writing. Most importantly, newly fluent writers seek feedback from others, as they know this is an essential part of their writing processes. Editing and revision are more fully appreciated as tools for improving a piece.

❖ ❖ ❖

Phases of writing development should *not* be confused with a gradual release of responsibility instructional framework. The four phases are indicators of where the student resides. The gradual-release instructional framework is a way of thinking about the instructional experiences of students, regardless of where they reside.

Likewise, the types of assessments collected serve two purposes. First, they offer evidence of the student's phase of writing development. Second, they provide information to teachers for making instructional decisions. Therefore, we see assessment as an important link between these two elements–the development of writers in a gradual release of responsibility model of instruction.

Writing Assessments: What Should Be Collected?

Similar to reading, writing can and should be assessed based on different components. In reading, we assess phonemic awareness, phonics knowledge, fluency, spelling, vocabulary knowledge, comprehension, and so on. In writing, we also should assess students on a number of dimensions.

Vicki Spandel and Richard Stiggins (1997) suggest that there are "six key qualities most often cited by teachers as significant." These six qualities, or attributes, are:

1. *ideas*

2. *organization*

3. *voice*

4. *word choice*

5. *sentence fluency*

6. *conventions*

These six qualities have come to be known as the "traits of writing." An additional trait for assessing polished pieces is the presentation, or appearance, of the piece (Culham, 2003).

HOLISTIC WRITING RUBRIC

9-POINT SCALE

9-8 Excellent paper. A 9 is reserved for papers that are nearly perfect in content, organization, mechanics, and language use. Both 8 and 9 are excellent papers in areas of form and content, with 9s being definitely of higher quality.

7 Still an excellent paper, but not quite so well organized, creative, and articulate.

6-5 An adequate paper, deficient in its organization, use of content, style, and/or mechanics.

4-3 A lower-half paper that is weak in content, organization, style, and/or mechanics.

2 A very weak paper that addresses the topic but is only loosely organized, with serious faults in organization, content, language use, style and mechanics.

1 A paper that addresses the topic but that is disorganized, inarticulate, and full of errors.

6-POINT SCALE

6-5 Excellent paper. A 6 is reserved for papers that are nearly perfect in content, organization, mechanics, and language use. Both 5 and 6 are excellent papers in areas of form and content, with 6s being definitely of higher quality.

4 A passing paper judged adequate in terms of content, organization, mechanics, and style. It may lack imagination and creativity.

3 A lower-half paper that is weak in content, organization, style, and/or mechanics.

2 A very weak paper that addresses the topic but is only loosely organized, with serious faults in organization, and mechanics.

1 A paper that addresses the topic but that is disorganized, inarticulate, and full of errors.

4-POINT SCALE

4 An excellent paper that is well-organized and displays facile use of language, content, and mechanics.

3 A paper that demonstrates adequate organization, content, language use, and handling of mechanics. It may lack imagination and creativity.

2 A lower-half paper that is weak in content, organization, style, and/or mechanics.

1 An unacceptable paper that addresses the topic but is weak in organization, content, and language use, and is full of errors in mechanics.

From "An Integrated Approach to the Teaching and Assessment of Language Arts" by D. Lapp, D. Fisher, J. Flood, and A. Cabello (in *Literacy Assessment of Second Language Learners*, S.R. Hurley and J.V. Tinajero, eds.). Copyright © 2001. Reprinted by permission of Allyn & Bacon.

As Spandel and Stiggins (1997) note, "writing is complex. It's part thought, part passion, and part structure." Thus our assessment tools must provide information for the teacher on each of these six key qualities. This can be accomplished with five types of tools: *holistic, attribute, analytic, timed,* and *self-assessments.* By using all of these approaches to assess writing, teachers, students, families, and communities can discuss writing more completely.

→ HOLISTIC ASSESSMENTS

In holistic assessments, students are given a numerical or qualitative score derived from the general impressions of a piece of writing. These types of assessment allow teachers to assess the entire piece through the use of a rubric, a scoring guide designed to evaluate otherwise subjective items. (The word *rubric* comes from the Latin word meaning "red," because this was the color of ink used to print directions to priests in religious books.) In a holistic assessment, the parts are not assessed separately. Teachers score the whole writing sample to determine if the piece works as a product. Holistic writing rubrics are useful for large-scale writing assessments, such as those used by states to measure the writing of all fourth through seventh graders. They are also useful for grade-level assessments given for the purposes of fostering discussion among teachers. An example appears on page 39.

→ ATTRIBUTE ASSESSMENTS

While these are often placed in the broad category of holistic assessments, we see them as differing in their characteristics and use. Attribute assessments are scored based on the objectives of the specific writing assignment. These general impressions are further defined by a series of attributes or traits. The aforementioned *6 + 1 Traits of Writing* is used widely by teachers as a way to define a series of attributes. This allows teachers to acknowledge the demands of the task, the time constraints, as well as the type of instruction that was provided when scoring the writing piece. As with a holistic assessment, a rubric is used. A continuum of performance levels is further defined in language that is observable and, in some cases, measurable. The rubric used by Ms. Abrams on page 30 is an example of an attribute writing rubric.

Because the traits of writing model is used by so many teachers, we think it is useful to look at attributes using this lens. Regardless of specific language, you will find that most attribute rubrics contain many of these elements.

IDEAS. This is the message or main idea of the piece. Considerations about the ideas include whether the main idea is interesting and whether the details selected to explain it are accurate and extend beyond what a reader would expect to be told.

ORGANIZATION. This attribute refers to the structure used by the writer. This includes text structures such as compare/contrast as well as purposes, such as the explanation of a procedure. Important considerations include whether the organization is logical and the extent to which all the ideas raised by the writer are addressed somewhere in the piece. For example, wouldn't you be frustrated if we told you we were going to do something in this chapter, then failed to do it?

VOICE. This is the personality of the writer, as evidenced by the use of humor, personal connections, and a quality that allows the reader to recognize that the piece could come from only one person. Think of your favorite writer; how do you recognize his or her work, beyond the topic? This is the writer's voice.

WORD CHOICE. Does the writer use language with precision? Does he or she vary words so that the same terms don't reappear excessively? Word choice is a reflection of the accuracy, variety, and precision of the vocabulary employed by the writer. Mark Twain may have said it best when he wrote, "The difference between the right word and the almost right word is the difference between *lightning* and *lightning bug*." (By the way, your sense that this is classic Twain is an indication of his use of voice in his writings.)

SENTENCE FLUENCY. This is a measure of how the sentences "hang together." Writers with good sentence fluency use sentences as a tool for pacing, such as when an action passage is described through fast, clipped sentences. Sentence fluency also refers to the ways in which the writer uses transitions and referents to carry the reader from one point to the next.

CONVENTIONS. This attribute is perhaps the most readily noticeable, because it concerns mechanics such as spelling, capitalization, punctuation, and grammar. Because this is so grounded in the writer's understanding of the way that the language works, it is necessary to adjust expectations according to the student's developmental level.

PRESENTATION. The way in which the piece appears on the page can influence the reader's ability to determine the message. Presentation includes handwriting, text features such as titles and headings, and illustrations, graphs, tables, or other visuals. (Notice that this trait does not appear in an attribute rubric that focuses on first-draft writing, such as the rubric shown in on page 30.)

RELATED SOURCES

There is extensive information available about the traits of writing. Ruth Culham's comprehensive guide *6 + 1 Traits of Writing* (Scholastic, 2003) is available for grades 3–6 and also K–2. For an online source, try the Northwest Regional Educational Laboratory's Web site at **http://www.nwrel.org/assessment/**. The rubrics provided are also available in Spanish.

When any attribute assessment is used, both the students and the teacher should understand the dimensions that are being evaluated. This means that the rubric must be used as a teaching tool, not as a yardstick that is revealed only after the writing is complete. We sometimes use a single attribute for teaching and assessment. A single attribute assessment rubric on position statements for evidence and examples is shown below.

Level 4	There are multiple examples to support the writer's point of view. The examples are accurate and consistent with the position offered by the writer.
Level 3	The writer provides a few examples to support his or her point of view. They are accurate but are not featured throughout the piece.
Level 2	There are only one or two examples to support the writer's point of view. While the example is accurate, it is not strong enough to persuade the reader.
Level 1	The piece has no examples, or the examples provided are inaccurate or misleading.

When providing specific instruction regarding an attribute, it's helpful to use the rubric to foster conversations with students about the characteristics of an element of writing.

→ ANALYTIC ASSESSMENTS

Another kind of writing assessment is the analytic protocol. An analytic assessment can be used to score writing according to quantitative measures, such as fluency and conventions. Fluency is typically recorded as the average number of words produced per minute. A common way to assess maturity is by determining the average number of words per sentence. As Brown (1973) noted in his work in oral language, the length of the utterance (in his case orally) reflected developmental sophistication. In other words, the longer the utterance, the more likely the child is to be older or more linguistically developed. Conventions also can be assessed by determining the average number of errors per sentence. For instance, Fearn and Farnan (2001) suggest counting the number of mechanical errors—spelling, capitalization, and punctuation—and dividing that number by the number of sentences. Other analytic assessments can include the number of sentences written, the overall number of words written, and the average sentence length. Ms. Abrams used an analytic protocol periodically to evaluate E. J.'s writing progress in fluency and average sentence length.

→ TIMED WRITING ASSESSMENTS

Analytic assessment data is frequently coupled with a holistic or attribute assessment to gain a picture of a student's writing that is both quantitative and qualitative in nature. An excellent way to look at the progress of a group of students over time in both dimensions is via timed writing prompts. During the first weeks of school, and about every six weeks thereafter, teachers at the schools where we work collect timed writing samples for analytic and attribute assessment. They establish a time limit (usually between 20 and 45 minutes, depending on the grade level) and administer the prompt on the same date. The prompts should include various genres and be age- and grade-level appropriate, for example:

- *Describe your ideal bedroom.*
- *Are school uniforms a good idea?*

- *My goals for sixth grade are. . . .*

- *Explain to a Martian how to make a peanut butter and jelly sandwich.*

- *Was Marty a sneaky boy? (based on a class reading of* **Shiloh***)*

Because they're timed, students have a common assessment experience across classrooms. These timed writing samples allow a grade level or a department to control for background knowledge while examining unedited, first-draft writing. After administering the assessment, students are asked to count the overall number of words and write it at the top of the first page. They also count the number of sentences in the piece. This is an important labor-saving step for teachers. The following steps are then employed:

1. The paper is first read for conventions. The number of errors in punctuation, capitalization, grammar, and spelling are recorded. You will recall from the earlier discussion on conventions that this should be measured according to grade-level expectations.

2. The analytic portion of the assessment is then calculated, including: number of words written, average sentence length, and average number of errors per sentence.

3. Papers are then traded with other teachers to be scored using either a holistic or attribute rubric. We trade papers with one another in order to take advantage of a fresh perspective. Since we evaluate our own students' writing for an entire school year, we see this as an opportunity for our students to write to a new reader.

4. The papers are returned to the classroom teacher for a second round of scoring. We have found that this phase of the process raises interesting and valuable questions among teachers about the attributes. We recall a very interesting conversation at an English department meeting among our colleagues who had discovered that they did not have full agreement on what constituted a good summary. Although these conversations can be disconcerting, they are incredibly important for our own teaching practices.

5. Classroom teachers bring examples of scored student work to the next grade-level or department meeting. In particular, we bring examples that show a range of mastery. The focus of the conversation is on how these inform our teaching.

STUDENT SELF-ASSESSMENT

Name: _____ Date: _____

Title: _____

Please complete this and attach it to your assignment.

Yes   No   *Explain*

❑   ❑   Did you understand the assignment? _____
            _____

❑   ❑   What was hard for you? _____
            _____

❑   ❑   What was easy for you? _____
            _____

❑   ❑   How did you help yourself? _____
            _____

❑   ❑   Is there anything you wished you had gotten help for? _____
            _____

❑   ❑   What do you think is the best feature of this piece? _____
            _____

Circle the words you think your readers will use to describe your piece:

funny	fascinating	exciting
sad	confusing	boring
moving	touching	challenging
surprising	thought-provoking	inspiring
interesting	puzzling	humdrum

INDIVIDUAL STUDENT ASSESSMENT PROFILE

Name: _____ Teacher: _____

	MONTH 1	MONTH 2	MONTH 3	MONTH 4	MONTH 5	PLANS FOR NEXT SEMESTER
Analytic:						
Words per minute						
Words per sentence						
Errors per sentence						
Attributes:						
Ideas						
Organization						
Voice						
Word Choice						
Sentence Fluency						
Conventions						
Presentation						
Timed Writing Results						
Self-Assessment						

Conference Notes:

CLASS SUMMARY INFORMATION

Grade: _____ School Year: _____ from _____ to _____

Student	Words per Minute (WPM)	Sentence Length	Errors per Sentence	Attributes Score	Holistic Score

Next steps for teaching: _____

_____

Of course, this same process can be used by a single teacher. However, we encourage you to think about partnering with a colleague to evaluate your students' writing. These conversations can reveal important insights into the teaching and learning going on in our classrooms.

→ STUDENT SELF-ASSESSMENT

In this type of assessment, students respond to a series of questions about a piece of their own writing. Questions focus on their perception of a piece, such as "What do you think is the best feature of your piece?" These self-assessments can also form the basis for a writing conference with the teacher. We ask students to complete a self-assessment and attach it to major writing projects. Naturally, this student self-reported information is compared with the holistic, attribute, and/or analytic assessments used for the assignment, as well as observations of the other students in class. We have included one of ours on page 45.

Addressing the Paperwork Burden: Data Collection and Recordkeeping Tools

By now, you're probably asking yourself how you'll remember all the assessment information for each of your students. You are also probably thinking, "Where will I store all of this stuff?" To us, this means that you understand the powerful role that writing assessment will play in your writing instruction. However, we don't want to minimize the logistical challenges associated with writing assessments.

As the Individual Student Profile tool on page 46 shows, writing assessment information can be summarized each semester for a single student on a single sheet of paper. The student summary form also guides assessment data collection during the school year. We use this chart to remind ourselves about when data needs to be collected. As an organizer, it alerts us to gaps that we have in our portrait of a student. In addition, it's a way to determine rapidly where progress is being made (or isn't). We use this chart as a tool for a midyear review, as well. By providing a history of the student's achievement, it can also inform the next teacher. This record allows the teacher to start the new year off with sound information upon which to plan instruction.

In addition to the individual student summary information, a teacher can summarize key pieces of assessment information for the whole class. (See page 47.) This information allows the teacher to make instructional decisions for the whole class, small groups of students, and individuals. As you can see from the example from Ms. Allen's fifth-grade class, she has made a number of instructional decisions based on this information. In particular, she noticed that many of her students were writing short sentences, and she wanted to increase their ability to write more complex sentences, so she decided to focus her generative sentences lessons on compound sentences.

Using these tools to maintain records of assessment information helps teachers plan instruction in ways that make a difference for students. They allow teachers to determine how much support is needed versus how much control students can handle, which is the heart of the gradual-release model. These tools can also help teachers plan which instructional strategies you will use with the whole class and which strategies should be used with small groups and individual students.

Grade: 5		School Year: 2003-04	From 9/15 to 10/13		
	WPM	Sent. Lgth.	Errors per sentence	Attributes Score	Holistic Score
Adriana	27	6	1	2	3
Martha	22	5	2	2	2
Naikeli	21	7	2	2	2
Tino	32	11	1	3	4
Leo	31	10	1	3	5
Jorge	23	8	2	2	3
Edgar	18	7	3	1	2
Eduardo	22	6	2	2	3
Naira	28	9	2	3	4
Mariah	34	11	2	3	5
Jessica	31	10	3	2	3
Ivette	16	5	4	1	2
Jose	29	8	3	2	3
Jesus	26	7	3	2	3
Miriam	25	8	2	2	3
Alejandra	22	7	5	2	2
Karen	36	12	1	4	5
Robert	30	9	2	3	3
David	24	6	5	2	3
Anahi	31	10	3	3	4

Providing Students Feedback (Without Tears)

In addition to the records you maintain to plan instruction, you must also provide students with feedback about their writing. This is part of your assessment responsibility and directly relates to the instruction that students require to become successful writers.

We recently observed a well-meaning teacher provide feedback to a student about her writing. The teacher was thoughtful in her comments and provided the student with specific information to improve the piece. But within the first few minutes of the interaction, the student was in tears. Through her sobs, she muttered, "I, I, I . . . tried my best."

Unfortunately, we have all been in this situation. Writing is very personal, and we have ego investments in what we write. As Fearn and Farnan note, "Writers write as well as they can every time they write, knowing that in the draft, the best they can do is an approximation of what their best looks like after their revision" (2001). The implications that students write as well as they can suggests to us that teachers must use gentle editing. We don't mean that teachers should overlook mistakes, but rather that they should focus on an instructional goal of talking with students about their papers. Further, we know that teachers must create an environment in which students are allowed to make mistakes and to learn from those mistakes. This cannot simply be the rule during writing—students must feel safe to take risks and learn from errors throughout the day if they are to do this with something as personal as writing.

Having said that, we support both peer feedback and writing conferences as tools to ensure that students receive feedback. Naturally, these structures must be taught and used regularly to be effective. Let's examine peer response first.

PEER RESPONSE

We don't want peers to perform only the functions of an editor. In fact, our experience has been that students are much better equipped to serve as thoughtful readers. They must be taught how to provide helpful feedback to ensure that peer-response work is a good use of instructional time. Jay Simmons' noteworthy work in the venue of peer response to writing offers guidance. We've used his system for categorizing types of responses that are helpful to fellow writers (see page 51). These responses include the following:

GLOBAL PRAISE. We want students to deliver praise to one another. After all, peer relationships outside the writing conference can be positively affected by the interactions that occur during this time. We develop a range of praises we can offer one another about our writing. It is not a matter of being insincere; it is a matter of being sensitive to the feelings of others.

PERSONAL RESPONSE. Interacting with a classmate's writing should provoke peer readers to wonder about the writer and his or her experiences. In turn, peer readers can ask questions that raise important points for writers; when the reader asks the writer about his or her experiences or why the topic was selected, the writer may think about his or her piece in a different way.

TYPES OF PEER RESPONSES

TYPE OF RESPONSE	DEFINITION	EXAMPLE
Global praise	Intended to make the writer feel good about his or her work.	"This is a great paper."
Personal response	Focuses on involvement of the writer as a person, not as a writer.	"Did this really happen to you?"
Text playback	Focuses on ideas or organization of the text.	"I think you wrote an excellent conclusion."
Sentence edits	Focuses on one or more sentences or grammar.	"This is a run-on sentence."
Word edits	Focuses on the use of words or spelling.	"You used this phrase too many times. Maybe you should try another one."
Reader's needs	Focuses on needs or reactions of the reader.	"This part is confusing to me."
Writer's strategies	Focuses on facilitating the writer's work by discussing the techniques that were used or could be used.	"In the fourth paragraph you get to the 'meat' of the experience. What if you didn't tell this in chronological order?"

Adapted from "Responders Are Taught, Not Born" by J. Simmons. Copyright © 2003 by J. Simmons. Reprinted by permission of the *Journal of Adolescent and Adult Literacy*.

TEXT PLAYBACK. One of the most helpful ways peers can help one another is to give the author feedback about a specific section of the text. Commentary about the title, conclusion, or choice of words is invaluable.

SENTENCE EDITS. We said before that we don't see students in the role of editors. This doesn't mean that they can't give feedback about simple things they may notice about a sentence. This can include conventions, grammar, or incomplete sentences.

WORD EDITS. Readers will sometimes notice spelling errors as well. If they notice something, they should say so.

TECHNIQUES TO TEACH PEER RESPONSES

TECHNIQUE	WHAT THE TEACHER DOES	WHAT STUDENTS DO
Share your writing	Share a piece of writing and ask for responses.	Offer comments on the teacher's writing.
Clarify evaluation versus response	Show that evaluation is a product, while response is to the writer.	Understand that response is personable and helpful.
Model specific praise	Show how you tell a writer what you like as a reader.	Learn that "cheerleading" is too general to be helpful.
Model understanding	Restate the meaning of the piece.	Learn that reflecting back the piece to the writer is helpful.
Model questions	Create questions about what you don't understand.	Learn that questions help the writer clarify his or her purpose.
Model suggestions	Clarify writing techniques.	Appreciate that a responder leaves a writer knowing what to do next.
Comment review	Read the comments of peers to writers.	Get teacher feedback on comments.

Adapted from "Responders Are Taught, Not Born" by J. Simmons. Copyright © 2003 by J. Simmons. Reprinted by permission of the *Journal of Adolescent and Adult Literacy.*

READER'S NEEDS. This is our favorite part of the peer-response process. The conversation should involve the reader's understanding of the piece, including parts that were exciting or interesting, as well as any areas of confusion.

WRITER'S STRATEGIES. This is the place where fellow writers can discuss strategies. These are always viewed as suggestions, and an author is free to apply or disregard suggestions.

Not every peer conference involves all these elements. After teaching each kind of response, we let authors decide whether they'd like to get that particular peer response from a reader. This reduces hurt feelings and misunderstandings. Strategies for teaching students to become skilled responders to their peers' papers are included in chart above and addressed again in Chapter 8.

→ WRITING CONFERENCES

The last component of our assessment portrait is the writing conference. These meetings occur between the teacher and the young writer and typically focus on one or more pieces. The intent of the writing conference is to understand more fully the processes used and perceptions held by the writer. In addition, the conference can result in information for use in future instructional lessons. We've included the general writing conference form we use when meeting with students and tips for using it in Chapter 8 (see pages 137–140).

Ms. Abrams used a similar format for her writing conferences when she met with E. J. Here are some excerpts from their conference:

Ms. Abrams: Hi, E. J. Welcome to your October writing conference. We've done this before, so you know that this is a way for us to talk about your writing.

E. J.: Yep. I brought stuff.

Ms. Abrams: Great! Tell me about what you have.

E. J.: I brought my journal. I wanted to show it to you.

For the next few minutes, E. J. shows Ms. Abrams his journal, and she turns the pages and asks some general questions about his thinking. Ms. Abrams determines that while E. J. wants to be a better writer, he is unsure of how to accomplish this. She returns to her conference form to guide her questioning.

Ms. Abrams: E. J., what kinds of writing do you like to do best?

E. J.: Well... I don't know. Maybe when we write stuff about animals and stuff.

Ms. Abrams: Tell me more about that. What do you like about it?

E. J.: I guess I like it 'cause I know lots.

Ms. Abrams: That makes sense to me.

E. J.: Yeah, animals.

Ms. Abrams: Are there special words you use when you write about animals?

E. J.: Yeah, you know in books, like science books? They use the names of the animals, and sometimes they have more than one name.

Ms. Abrams: Why do you think that's important?

E. J.: Well, sometimes animals have different names in different parts of the world. Like cougars. They're called mountain lions, and pumas, and panthers. They're all the same animal.

Ms. Abrams: Wow! That sounds like something you could write about. It sounds like you know a lot.

E. J.: And there's only about fifty left of the Florida panthers.

Ms. Abrams: What if you wrote about cougars? What would you need to help you?

E. J.: Well, I know a lot. But I might need to go to the library.

Ms. Abrams: We can do that. Let's make a plan for you to go to the school library to get some books about cougars. Could you use some other help from me?

E. J.: There's a lot about cougars. I might need help figuring out what to put in the report.

Ms. Abrams: I can definitely help with that. How about if you go to the library this morning to get a few books on cougars? Not too many—let's say three.

E. J.: Okay, and I'll read them.

Ms. Abrams: Since you know a lot, I'll bet you can skim them. Let's plan on talking about your cougar report again on Thursday for a few minutes so we can make a plan.

E. J.: Okay. Can I go to the library now?

This conference took less than ten minutes, but Ms. Abrams accomplished quite a bit. She had a chance to listen to E. J. talk about his writing and through her questioning gained some insight into his interests. She got him talking about a specific topic and helped him to formulate a plan for getting started. In addition, she also made plans with him for next steps as well as a follow-up meeting. Used in conjunction with the many other types of assessments we have discussed in this chapter, writing conferences are an effective way to promote conversation with students about their writerly lives.

Writing assessment is an important component of writing instruction. The information you gather from reviewing student work and talking with and observing students will allow you to plan instruction that makes a difference in their achievement. There are effective systems that can be established for maintaining the assessment information you collect. Further, there are systems that can be established to teach students to provide feedback to their peers and for you, the teacher, to provide feedback.

Now that you're armed with good assessment information, you're ready to teach! The remainder of the book focuses on the instructional strategies that allow you to gradually release responsibility for writing to your students. Each of these chapters includes other assessment information related to the instructional strategy profiled.

Language Experience Approach (LEA)

OBJECTIVE: To build speech-to-print connections

ACTIVITY: Students discuss a topic and agree on a written message that the teacher records.

LEVEL OF SUPPORT: Extensive

INSTRUCTIONAL FORMAT: Whole class, small groups, or individual students

Traditionally used in a one-on-one setting with emergent or struggling readers and English language learners, LEA is a technique for reinforcing the connections between speech and print. The teacher solicits the experiences of a student by engaging him or her in a conversation. As the student talks, the teacher scribes, writing down the story so the student can view it. In this way the LEA event provides students with information about how language is represented in written form. In our work with writers, LEA becomes a means for modeling the complex aspects of writing such as planning the layout of the message and applying conventions of print. Unlike the traditional approach, we use LEA in whole- and small-group lessons, as well as with individual students.

LEA is an important first step in writing instruction for two reasons. First, it's especially useful when assessment information indicates that students do not understand the speech-to-print connection and when they don't understand the different registers of language and the more complex language used in writing. In other words, LEA is highly indicated when students do not understand how to record their thoughts or spoken conversation. Writing effectively requires an understanding of the relationship between the spoken and the written word. Remember that students have a higher spoken than written vocabulary. They also think about things that are more complex than they can write. Without support and teaching, the writing becomes formulaic and uninspired because students continue to rely on a limited number of topics and styles.

Second, the Language Experience Approach is useful when students are uncomfortable writing in front of their peers. We find that many adolescents have never experienced academic success with writing or done writing they care about in school. They may also have had unsupportive or negative feedback on their writing from teachers. Consequently, these students are often unwilling to demonstrate their writing skills in front of the class. This may also be true for students learning English or those with learning disabilities.

While students may struggle to write, we must remember—and show them!—that they have interesting and profound thoughts to share. Students of all ages are interested in discussing their life experiences and the experiences they share together in class. As students become convinced that they will be respected in their interactions with peers and teachers, they become more willing to share their writing with others. LEA is one way to help change students' attitudes toward writing.

Features of a Language Experience Approach Lesson

In the Language Experience Approach, the writing done in class initially is teacher controlled: The teacher scribes almost everything while teaching bits and pieces of language structures and conventions to students. Teaching in context this way draws on students' experiences and thoughts to form the curriculum—an authentic and powerful approach to writing instruction that is echoed in the other approaches in our framework, as well.

A typical LEA sequence begins with a conversation about a specific topic. The teacher moves the discussion to a key point on which students agree and then scribes this message as students watch. The teacher may also focus instruction on some aspect of language or writing (mechanics, spelling, grammar, vocabulary, and so on) in the discussion. Once the teacher writes the agreed-upon message—either on a dry erase board, chalkboard, or chart paper so everyone can easily see it—he or she can ask students to do any of the extension activities shown on page 57. The choice of activity depends on students' familiarity with LEA, their understanding of and comfort with text, and the time the teacher has set aside for writing instruction.

FOLLOW-UP ACTIVITIES

- *Reread previous LEA text messages. This reinforces the speech-to-print connections that students need to develop.*

- *Copy the LEA message into a journal. This requires that students become writers of complex text even if they cannot produce it independently.*

- *Illustrate the LEA message. This allows students to demonstrate their comprehension of the message.*

- *Add two thoughts to the agreed-upon message. This gives students the chance to extend the message and connect their thinking with the rest of the class.*

ASSESSMENT LINK

Speaking in front of others is a skill that students must develop. As a teacher, you may want to focus on one or two students during the Language Experience Approach lesson and collect some assessment information about their public speaking efforts. An assessment tool for this can be found on page 58. You'll note that there are four opportunities to assess the student on the same set of skills. This will allow you to determine the amount of growth during the school year. Note also that this assessment tool can be used for instructional planning. If several students are having difficulty with taking turns or speech volume, you can plan appropriate instruction for them.

Using Language Experience Approach With the Whole Class

Mr. Mongrue is using LEA with his eighth-grade students to model writing and to help them see themselves as writers. The majority of students in his English class are English language learners, although about 30 percent are native speakers. However, few of them write at or near grade level. Mr. Mongrue has noticed, however, that they are talkers and thinkers.

A few weeks after the attacks of September 11, 2001, he hears them

SPEAKING CHECKLIST

Name: _____

When _____ speaks
in a group, he/she:

DATES

sticks to the topic.				
builds support for the subject.				
speaks clearly.				
takes turns and waits to talk.				
talks so others in the group can hear.				
speaks smoothly.				
uses courteous language.				
presents in an organized and interesting way.				
supports the topical thesis.				
answers questions effectively.				
is comfortable speaking publicly.				
maintains listeners' interest.				
volunteers to answer in class.				

Adapted from "An Integrated Approach to the Teaching and Assessment of Language Arts" by D. Lapp, D. Fisher, J. Flood, and A. Cabello (in *Literacy Assessment of Second Language Learners*, S. R. Hurley and J. V. Tinajero, eds.). Copyright © 2001. Printed by permission of Allyn & Bacon.

expressing sophisticated thoughts and raising difficult questions. It's the first month of school, and most students have been reluctant to engage in extended writing, let alone in sharing their writing with others. From past experience, Mr. Mongrue knows that LEA can be an effective tool for moving past the resistance of struggling adolescent writers.

He begins a shared reading of a newspaper article about the children who were orphaned following the attacks. While he reads aloud the article, all the students can see the print either on their own copy or on the overhead. Then a smaller group of students discusses the title of the article, "Children of the Dead." Marquis is the first to speak. He tells of his father's death in a "drug deal gone bad." He asks if he is also one of the children of the dead.

Mr. Mongrue answers, "You've posed an interesting question, and I'm going to write it here on the board." He writes: *Are children left behind from drug deals gone bad also the children of the dead?*

"Let's go back to the article," Mr. Mongrue suggests. "The subtitle is 'Consoling Offspring Is Priority.' Do you know the word *consoling*?"

Isabel answers, "It means comforting or hugging."

"Great—What about the word *offspring*?" Mr. Mongrue asks. When none of the students give an answer, he explains that *offspring* means a parent's child or children. He offered an example: "I'll use it in a sentence. I am my parents' offspring." Then Mr. Mongue asks students to add the word to their vocabulary journals while he makes a note to himself to include it on the word wall.

When he is sure that the vocabulary is clear, Mr. Mongrue poses questions about students' reaction to the text. "I'm going to write down some of the things you say," he tells them. "So, I'm wondering, what did you think about when we read this article?"

Flordida is the first to answer: "I can't imagine what it must be like for those kids." Mr. Mongrue writes her statement on the board.

Fernando adds, "It's wrong, and I'm angry. I want them to pay."

Mr. Mongrue writes these sentences and asks for clarification. "Fernando, who are you talking about when you say, 'I want them to pay'?"

"The terrorists," Fernando replies. Mr. Mongrue erases the word *them* and replaces it with *the terrorists*. "You've used an interesting expression: 'to pay.' I assume you don't mean money. Let's talk about that idea."

For the next several minutes, the class discusses the feelings of vengeance being experienced by so many Americans. Several students make connections to the story about the children of the victims. Mr. Mongrue writes particularly powerful statements on the board as the students speak. Within a few minutes, he has written these statements on the board:

- *Are children left behind from drug deals gone bad also the children of the dead?*

- *I can't imagine what it must be like for those kids.*

- *It's wrong, and I'm angry. I want the terrorists to pay.*

- *The terrorists will pay for their actions.*

- *The children must be confused and so mad at the world.*

- *What can the families tell the children about why it happened?*

"Now you've got a lot of ideas on the board," Mr. Mongrue says. "Let's read them over and make some decisions about how we're going to use them to start our journal writing."

As he reads aloud the statements, he also comments on his decisions to use conventions such as capitalization and punctuation, modeling how writers integrate decisions about conventions in their writing.

After much discussion, students agree to extend the first sentence: *The terrorists will pay for their actions.*

Mr. Mongue also is able to use the word *action* to focus students' attention on the common spelling pattern *–tion*. He asks students to scan the article for other words that end in *–tion*. Students find the words *negotiation*, *generation*, and *operation*, which Mr. Mongrue also writes on the board.

Finally, he asks students to copy the agreed-upon sentence in their writing journals. "Use this sentence as your first sentence in a paragraph. You can use any of these other statements as well, or none at all. What I want to see are several more sentences that relate to this idea," he instructs them.

Using Language Experience Approach With Small Groups

Ms. Riley has selected the picture book *The Jazz Fly* by Matthew Gollub for all her third-grade students to listen to at a listening post. As students listen to the author speak and sing on the CD, they follow along in the book.

Then a group of three students—Mario, Jessica, and Angel—excitedly join Ms. Riley for a Language Experience Approach lesson. She has formed this temporary group because she has observed that these three students often have difficulty getting started with their writing. For instance, just the other day, she noticed Mario staring off into the distance while other students were busy writing. When she prompted him to get started, Mario rather indignantly replied, "I'm thinking!" Ms. Riley has planned a writing activity for the whole class, but she expects these three students will need extra support to get them going. Here is an excerpt of their dialogue:

Ms. Riley: You're all going to be writing about *The Jazz Fly* tomorrow. Let's talk about the story and what you noticed. As you talk, I'm going to write down some of your ideas. Later, we'll look at these ideas so you can use one or two to start your own writing. Let's start by retelling the story.

Angel: The Jazz Fly made this sound: *ZA-baza, BOO-zaba, ZEE-zah RO-ni.*

Mario and Jessica: *ZA-baza, BOO-zaba, ZEE-zah RO-ni!*

Ms. Riley: I'll write that down. We can use the book to make sure we spell those sounds the right way. (She writes: *The Jazz Fly says ZA-baza, BOO-zaba, ZEE-zah RO-ni.*)

Jessica: He was late for a gig.

Ms. Riley: Okay, I'll write that, too: *He was late for a gig.* That sounds like a sentence from the book. Were you able to figure out what a *gig* was?

Jessica: Yeah, it's like a show… a music show.

(Ms. Riley continues to write their statements on a chart, pausing once to say, "You're getting quite a few ideas written down here." At one point in the conversation and retelling, students make a connection to their own experiences.)

Mario: That pig didn't know how to tell the fly where to go.

Angel: But the dog helped.

Jessica: Yeah, the dog helped. He got there … got to the show.

Mario: One time, I got lost and my mom couldn't find me.

TIP

Center Activities Rotation System (CARS)

A key to small-group instruction is grouping according to need. Since needs change, the composition of groups must change as well. The Center Activity Rotation System developed by Flood & Lapp is a grouping strategy that allows the teacher to meet with small groups of students who are selected for their instructional needs while the rest of the class works at collaborative learning centers. Do this in your classroom by creating heterogeneous groups for centers and then calling individuals from multiple groups for direct instruction. This management system ensures that students are not permanently grouped by ability.

(LAPP, FLOOD, & GOSS, 2000).

Jessica: Me too, I got lost too.

Ms. Riley: Who helped you? How were you found?

Jessica: Well, I had to ask somebody. I had to get some help.

Mario: I had to get help from an adult.

Ms. Riley: Is there a message we should remember about our experiences and the experiences that the fly had?

Mario: If you get lost, ask for help.

Angel: Yeah, when you're lost, ask for help.

Ms. Riley: Let's make that into a very important sentence: *When you're lost, ask for help.*

(The students talk for a few more minutes about whom to ask for help. As the conversation comes to a close, Ms. Riley reminds them of their assignment.)

Ms. Riley: Tomorrow you're going to write about *The Jazz Fly*. You've got lots of good sentences here to use in your writing. You might even be able to use one as a start to your writing. I'm going to keep this chart paper for you. If you get stuck, I want you to look at our work today to help get yourself unstuck.

USING LANGUAGE EXPERIENCE APPROACH WITH INDIVIDUAL STUDENTS

David is a newcomer to Ms. Allen's fifth-grade class. Having arrived from Mexico earlier in the school year, he is also new to schooling in the United States. All the students in David's class are bilingual in Spanish and English. David, however, is concerned about his ability to write in English since he's had very little formal education in the conventions of written English.

To address this need, Ms. Allen meets daily with David for a short LEA lesson. They start the lessons with David reading some of the pages in his writing journal that contain previous LEA lessons. Rereading these familiar sentences helps him process written English. Once David has read a few selected texts, he and Ms. Allen have a conversation. This individual time is important for David's writing development and his self-esteem. By her close attention to his words—spoken and written—Ms. Allen communicates that he is a valued member of the class.

One day, David reveals that he wants to go to college. When Ms. Allen asks him about this, David says that he knows she is in college and he wants to go too. Ms. Allen has spoken often to her class about her work in a master's program at the local university. David says that he hasn't found a book about college but that the librarian has said that she will help him locate some. In the meantime, David is reading *I Got a D in Salami* by Henry Winkler and Lin Oliver because he likes the main character Hank and relates to the trouble Hank has in school. Ms. Allen begins a discussion of the book with David.

"What parts of the book have you liked best?" she asks.

"The part where he... he... got his report card in the meat grinder. I wish that sometimes, too!" David responds.

"Why do you wish that?" Ms. Allen queries. She recognizes that this statement might be an invitation to discuss matters closer to David's heart.

"He got bad grades... *D*s in his classes. In spelling. I work hard on spelling but I don't do very well," David replies slowly.

Ms. Allen nodded. "I remember that part of the story. What happened to Hank again? At the spelling bee?"

"He study his words really hard," David tells her. "But he lost the first word. He spell it wrong."

"Yes, he spelled that first word wrong and he was out of the spelling bee." Ms. Allen restates his comments, using more conventional syntax. "Has something like that happened to you?"

"Well, no, but I got bad grades on my spelling test," David answers.

"Was it like Hank's situation? Did you study hard?" Ms. Allen suspects she knows the answer to this question. David, a bright student, did well in school in Mexico. However, he didn't develop strong study habits there, which is hurting him now.

David lowers his eyes. "Not really," he admits.

Then Ms. Allen asks David what he needs to do to get into college. David talks about passing high school, getting money together, moving to college, and the like. At one point, he says that he needs to stay focused on education. Ms. Allen asks David to repeat the sentence. He says, "I must stay focused on my education if I want to get ahead." Ms. Allen writes this sentence in David's journal and asks him to read it aloud. The words and ideas "stay focused,"

> I must stay focused on my education if I want to get ahead. I want to go to collage. I will help me for my life.

"education," and "get ahead" will all be rich material to return to as they move forward in their LEA work together.

Following this individualized lesson, Ms. Allen has David return to his desk and illustrate the sentence so he can remember what it said. She also reminds him to independently reread several of the pages from his writer's notebook.

Background on Research

The use of Language Experience Approach dates back more than 40 years. This instructional strategy was developed by Sylvia Ashton-Warner to foster reading among young Maori children. She asserted that the key vocabulary of each child was unique and personally meaningful. Ashton-Warner advocated for the use of this idiosyncratically meaningful language and reported that the stories developed out of LEA sessions provided her students with authentic materials that would otherwise exceed their capacity to read.

LEA was soon applied in many other types of classrooms around the world. Teachers engaged in the act of writing with and in front of children, noted that these materials were motivating and readable, regardless of traditional reading level evaluations (Dixon-Nessel, 1983; Stauffer, 1970). LEA has been shown to be effective with such seemingly diverse groups as bilingual kindergartners (Clark, 1995), reluctant middle school social studies students (Sharp, 1989), adults living in poverty in El Salvador (Purcell-Gates & Wateman, 2000), and elderly people who had not previously learned to read (Brehaut, 1994).

Educators and researchers were quick to notice that LEA, originally devised as an instructional strategy for reading, had a positive effect on writing as well. As early as 1975, LEA was being touted as a means for promoting writing, especially with older students (Britton, Burgess, Martin, McLeod, & Rosen, 1975). Perez (2000) noted that second language learners applied principles of writing such as planning and revision through exposure to LEA practices. Similarly, Karnowski (1989) documented the use of this instructional strategy to teach elementary students about the processes used by writers.

It appears that LEA is effective for students with disabilities as well. Ewoldt and Hammermeister (1989) used LEA to foster skills with students who were deaf. Gately (2004) used a case study approach to describe the effectiveness of LEA as a method for teaching the concept of words to students with significant disabilities. Taken together, the results of these writing studies are analogous to those conducted for reading. Given the essential nature of reading-writing connections, LEA is an excellent example of an instructional strategy that strengthens both.

KEY POINTS
FOR THE LANGUAGE EXPERIENCE APPROACH LESSON

The Language Experience Approach is perfect for introductory writing instruction, especially when students have not developed skills in recognizing the speech-to-print connection or if they are shy about writing in front of their peers.

To be effective, the LEA lesson should include:

- *conversation about a specific topic related to the student's experiences*

- *books or other texts connected to the lesson*

- *an agreed-upon text message written by the teacher*

- *student engagement in extension activities in which they use the LEA text*

Interactive Writing

OBJECTIVE: To compose collaboratively written messages based on group conversations

ACTIVITY: Students share the pen with their teacher and peers to construct a message.

LEVEL OF SUPPORT: Significant

INSTRUCTIONAL FORMAT: Whole class, small groups, or individual students

In interactive writing, the teacher and students plan and compose a written message based on a conversation or discussion. Once the content of the message is agreed upon, the teacher coaches individual students to write the message publicly. Depending on the developmental level of the writers, the message may be constructed letter by letter or in words and phrases. The result is a collaboratively written message that bears the handwriting of many students. These messages are typically short in length—third graders who are struggling with writing may compose only a few sentences during one lesson. However, the emphasis of interactive writing is on the richness of the lesson, rather than the overall length of the written message. It is truly an approach that values quality over quantity.

Interactive writing bears some resemblance to the Language Experience Approach in that the source of the content emanates from the students' experiences, but the attention is on the many decisions writers make to get their messages onto paper. These decisions may range from determining the content of the sentence, letter formation, planning the layout on the page, punctuation, and spelling.

As each student writer adds a letter or word to the message, the rest of the class repeats the entire message. This mimics the internal repetition writers use to keep syntax and meaning intact as they write a sentence. Because students now scribe each word on the board, the teacher can focus on teaching elements of written language, from conventions of print to clarity of message. Thus, language lessons are based on students' thinking and speech, and the instructional value of interactive writing lies in the development of oral language in students.

Since students take control of the pen, interactive writing can test the level of trust in the classroom. Any threat of embarrassment in front of peers can undermine a lesson, so it's essential that students view their mistakes as an opportunity for everyone to learn. The teacher is responsible for building this atmosphere of collaboration. Deep knowledge of students' control of words and vocabulary, and especially their understanding of structural analysis, is vital to a successful interactive writing lesson.

Features of an Interactive Writing Lesson

Implementation: Interactive writing is typically based on a book that the class has read, a shared experience the class has had, or a theme or topic that the class is studying, for example:

- **Shared reading:** *A third-grade class reads* Stellaluna *by Janell Cannon and writes a list of the characteristics of a bat.*

- **Content lesson:** *A fifth-grade class studying electricity and magnetism composes an explanation of how a compass works.*

- **Shared experience:** *A seventh-grade class creates a letter of thanks to the curator of the art museum they visited on a field trip.*

The teacher begins by establishing a purpose for the writing. In order for the writing to be authentic, students must perceive it as being composed for a reason beyond mere compliance. Once the purpose is established, the teacher helps the class determine the format for the writing and points out that the choice of format will dictate writing decisions as the class commits the message to paper.

Next, the teacher moves to a discussion of the topic. As previously mentioned, the importance of this phase of the lesson is on oral lan-

TIP

Challenges

- We've noticed that teachers who are new to the interactive writing process tend to overlook the importance of the discussion. In the rush to arrive at an agreed-upon message, a teacher may inadvertently short-change the opportunity for students to engage in a meaningful discussion of the topic. As with LEA, you want students to be fully invested in the words and ideas they will work with in their message.

- Another challenge of interactive writing instruction is the adaptability demands on a teacher. This process requires the teacher to constantly recognize the string of "teachable moments" found in the confusions and insights of young writers. Since students compose the message, the teacher cannot decide in advance exactly what the message will say—the message should come from the rich discussion at the beginning of the lesson. This doesn't mean that planning isn't necessary. To the contrary, the teacher must consider exactly what common experience to create in order to have something interesting to discuss.

guage development. Partner talk is effective for increasing the level of participation among all students. In addition, it invites the use of academic vocabulary as students hear and practice the language of the topic.

After discussing the subject and reaching a satisfactory level of understanding among students, the teacher helps them refine the message. This includes asking students to revisit the purpose of the message and to consider the audience for the piece. The teacher invites oral composition of a proposed opening sentence. The proposed sentences are discussed, debated, and refined—perhaps through word choice or the addition of a dependent clause.

Once a consensus is reached, the teacher writes the sentence on a note pad to remember the exact wording. Students rehearse the message aloud to reinforce content and wording. (Teachers of younger writers often count the words in the sentence as well. This is useful for planning the placement of words on the page, since many students struggle with squeezing in words along the right margin.)

Then the writing of the message begins. The teacher repeats the first word of the message and inquires about the first letter or the spelling of the entire word. The point here is to attend to the teaching points that will benefit students. The teacher calls on a volunteer to write the first letter, word, or phrase on a dry erase board, chalkboard, or chart paper, and checks to make sure the student is prepared to write. While he or she scribes, the teacher discusses an aspect of what is being written, including language conventions as we noted above.

When the first student finishes, the class reads aloud the written message thus far, *and* they repeat the rest of the message from memory. The teacher then calls on another student to continue writing the message and talks with the rest of the students. When this student finishes, the whole group reads the written text and again completes the part that is yet to be written. This proceeds until the entire message has been written.

Even when writers seem to be well prepared, mistakes happen. Of course, the goal is to get the message written correctly, but errors should be handled with sensitivity. Give assistance in either erasing the error (on a board) or covering it with a strip of white adhesive correction tape (on chart paper). Correction tape comes in a variety of widths from one to three feet and is available in most office and teaching supply stores and catalogs. The student can make the correction on the tape, which has a paper backing that's easy to write on.

Once the message is finished, the class rereads the entire message

ASSESSMENT LINK

It's important to note that the teacher selects students to write parts of the message based on the assessment information he or she has collected. The task should be reasonable and yet challenging enough for each student. This means that the teacher who uses interactive writing must understand what his or her students know and are ready to know. The assessment data gathered in other aspects of the literacy day are useful for these purposes.

Interactive writing can be used to assess:
- print conventions such as punctuation, capitalization, and text features
- developmental spelling assessments
- vocabulary knowledge
- grammar
- knowledge of processes of writing including idea generation, organization, voice, and elaboration

aloud and then discusses any improvements they can make. The teacher then introduces a follow-up activity or discusses the continuation of the message in the next lesson.

 ## FOLLOW-UP ACTIVITIES

After the interactive writing lesson, the teacher can ask students to do any of the extension activities below. The choice of activity depends on their understanding of and comfort with text and the time that's been set aside for writing instruction.

- *Reread previous interactive writing messages from saved chart papers. This reinforces the speech-to-print connections that students need to develop.*

- *Copy the message into a journal. Again, this requires that students become writers of complex text even if they cannot produce it independently.*

- *Illustrate the message. This allows students to demonstrate their comprehension of the message.*

- *Discuss the message with a partner to share perspectives orally. This is especially useful when students have composed a summary of information.*

- *Add two thoughts to the agreed-upon message. This allows students to extend the message and to connect their thinking with the whole class.*

 TIP

Classroom Management

While one student is writing the message, the other students need to be engaged as well. Here are some suggestions for brief teacher-directed activities that reinforce teaching points while a student is composing:

- Make a list of synonyms.
- Tell your partner other words that possess a characteristic in common with the target word (sound, spelling pattern, affix, or root word).
- Write a variation of the word on a response board.

Interactive Writing With the Whole Class

Mr. Steele's sixth-grade classroom is filled with thirty very excited English language learners. The students in this class have been in the United States for less than two years, and his instruction emphasizes spoken and written language.

One day, on the walk back from a science excursion to a nearby field, the students witness an accident between a man in a wheelchair and a car. Fortunately, the man is not injured, and the class waits with him and the driver until police arrive. When the students return to class, they animatedly debate the details of the accident, especially the sequence of events. Mr. Steele had hoped to write a summary of their observations in the field, but he soon realizes that the accident has distracted students from the science lesson. Although it is not the kind of traditional shared experience he usually plans for an interactive writing lesson, Mr. Steele recognizes the power of his students' interest in and concern about such an event. He settles down the class and suggests they write about the accident and try to figure out what they saw.

He is delighted with the outpouring of oral language that comes from these usually reluctant speakers. It seems that everyone has an opinion, and most are eager to share theirs. Some students claim that the man was already in the crosswalk. Others assert that he had entered the intersection carelessly. It soon becomes apparent that the class will not reach consensus.

"I'm not sure we're going to be able to agree," Mr. Steele tells them. "Let's get an opening sentence written together. Then I'm going to ask you to write what you saw."

There is one thing the class can agree upon—they disagree with one another. Wanese offers this observation, "We remember different."

"Yes, you're right. We certainly remember differently," replies Mr. Steele.

"No way. How could it be?" asks Gina. "We all saw the same thing."

"I'm hearing two very important ideas here. Wanese said that we remember things differently, even though Gina says we saw the same thing. Talk with your partner about a way you could put both of these ideas in the same sentence," Mr. Steele suggests.

His students are accustomed to partner talk and turn to one another to orally compose a sentence. After considering several suggestions, the class agrees that the best sentence is: *We all saw the same thing, but everyone remembers something different.*

Mr. Steele leads the class in a counting of the words, holding up his fingers as they chant the sentence. "Eleven words!" he exclaims. "We've got a lot to do! Who will be the first to write?"

Luis raises his hand. Mr. Steele asks Luis about the convention of using a capital letter to begin a sentence and then directs him to write the word on the dry erase board. As Luis finishes this word, the class repeat the entire message: *We all saw the same thing, but everyone remembers something different.*

After several students have written individual words of the message, Teleisia volunteers. This is her first time at the board, and the word she will write is *everyone*. She writes *Everyone*, capitalizing the word.

While Teleisia is doing this, Mr. Steele has the other students name other compound words that start with *every*. The class identifies *everything*, *everyday*, *everybody*, and *everywhere*. He reminds students to look at the word wall to help them. When Tarek notices the capitalization error, Mr. Steele asks for clarification on capitalizing nouns. Then Teleisia changes the word to *everyone,* and then the class repeats the entire message.

Tien writes the last word of the message. As he writes *different*, Mr. Steele tells students to write down a word that has the same letters next to each other. He does this in part to remind Tien that the word *different* has two *f*s. Students then share their words with partners, and their responses include *spelling*, *class*, *little*, and *book*. When Tien finishes, the whole class reads the complete message aloud: *We all saw the same thing, but everyone remembers something different.*

Following this whole-group activity, each student extends the class interactive writing message in his or her notebook. Oscar writes: *The car hit the wheelchair guy.* Luz Elena writes: *I saw the man go in the street and get hit. He did not look whin he crosed.*

Although this is not the way Mr. Steele had intended to spend instructional time, he is pleased with the level of oral language his students are working at. He also had a chance to discuss print conventions, sight words, and spelling patterns. In addition, the students used this interactive writing sentence as a start to their own original writing. A discussion of the science trip to the field could wait until the next day.

Interactive Writing With a Small Group

Ms. Alvarez knows that her third-grade students will pass notes to one another, just like she did when she was in school. She also knows that she can use their notes as a teaching and learning opportunity, so she encourages her students to write notes to one another regularly. Each student has a mailbox for receiving messages, notes, returned papers, and missed work, and students are expected to check their mailboxes regularly.

In addition, Ms. Alvarez has selected *Dear Mr. Blueberry* by Simon James as a way to engage her students with the idea that friends write letters to one another. As a class, they've read the story several times together, and Ms. Alvarez is ready to use it as a shared literary experience to reteach the format of friendly letters during small-group writing instruction.

She meets daily with small groups of students and has established a specific purpose for each group based on the needs of its members. These groups remain constant for approximately three weeks. At the end of the three-week rotation, she makes changes in the groups' membership.

The members of one group are having difficulty with letter writing, even though it was introduced earlier in the year. The assessment information Ms. Alvarez has collected about these students indicates that they can write. However, they don't know the correct format for letters, and they don't develop their ideas into paragraphs. Her spelling and fluency assessments indicate that the members of this group are near grade level. She's evaluated their work using the friendly letter rubric she developed, below.

After the group assembles, Ms. Alvarez asks the group to talk about the exciting events in *Dear Mr. Blueberry*. Here is an excerpt of their dialogue:

Charlotte: The girl had a whale in her pond!

Steve: Yeah, and her teacher didn't believe her.

(The other members of the group shake their heads in sympathetic disbelief at the idea that Mr. Blueberry would fail to believe his student, Emily.)

Ms. Alvarez: How did Emily communicate with her teacher?

Theresa: She wrote letters. It was summer vacation.

Ms. Alvarez: Let's look at those letters.

(They review the elements of a friendly letter and note that Emily and Mr. Blueberry used them all.)

CATEGORY	1	2	3
Greeting and signature	Missing greeting or signature	Has greeting and signature, but there are one or two mistakes	Correct greeting and signature
Format	Missing two or three elements (date, opening, closing sentence)	Missing one element	All elements in letter
Questions	Does not ask questions	Asks one question	Asks two or more questions
Grammar and spelling	Four or more mistakes	Two or three mistakes	No more than one mistake
Capitalization	Four or more mistakes	Two or three mistakes	No more than one mistake

Ms. Alvarez: Those things make a good friendly letter. I'd like for us to write a letter. It's fun to write a letter about something exciting. Can we think of something exciting that's happening in this class?

(They spend a few minutes of conversation about the lives of their classmates.)

Andrew: I know! Danny's mom is going to have a baby!

Heather: Yeah, we could write to Danny and tell him good luck.

Ms. Alvarez: That would be a great topic for a letter. What should come first in your letter?

Mike: The letter should begin with "Dear Danny."

(The students look hopefully at Ms. Alvarez, who has pulled a chart stand closer so that every member of the group can see.)

Ms. Alvarez: Okay, Mike, I'd like for you to write that on the chart paper. We'll read it again and decide if we're ready to go to the next sentence.

(Mike begins to write. Ms. Alvarez has noticed that they've forgotten the date but decides to wait to see if anyone else will pick up this omission. She doesn't have to wait long.)

Heather: Wait—aren't letters supposed to start with the date?

Mike: Oh, I forgot. (He adds the date to the top of the letter.)

Ms. Alvarez: Check the date on the board, Mike. That's a good way to help yourself.

(She knows she doesn't need to help Mike with the spelling of the date; she just needs to provide a bit of scaffolding to ensure it's done correctly.)

Ms. Alvarez: What should the opening sentence of the letter be?

Several possibilities are discussed, and the group settles on this sentence: *We are writing to congratulate you on your future baby brother or sister.* Given the needs of this group, Ms. Alvarez asks each member to write three words of the sentence on the chart paper. Andrew writes the first three words. Then the group reads aloud what he's written, as well as the remainder of the sentence from memory. As Heather writes the next three words, Ms. Alvarez discusses the pronouns used in the sentence. Heather finishes, and the group reads the sentence aloud, supplying the unwritten words from memory.

As the group continues to write the letter to Danny, Ms. Alvarez provides regular feedback about topic sentences and the detail sentences that follow. As possible sentences are proposed, she asks if they are related to the sentences already written. Soon the letter is finished, and Ms. Alvarez uses the rubric to evaluate the letter. Then she lets the students evaluate it.

Ms. Alvarez: We reread because sometimes we have to revise our writing. Will you read aloud the letter one more time for me?

(The students read the entire letter aloud and pronounce their work satisfactory. Ms. Alvarez agrees. She invites the group to talk about writing the letter and then to add illustrations to it. Soon the session comes to a close.)

Ms. Alvarez: We're going to continue writing letters this year. As you write, remember to use all these elements to make a great letter, like the ones Emily wrote to Mr. Blueberry!

During this first letter-writing session, Ms. Alvarez realizes that this group will need to work on paragraphing in greater detail, so she plans future small-group lessons based on this information.

Interactive Writing With an Individual Student

While most of the research on interactive writing is done with the whole class or small groups, this strategy can also be used effectively with individual students. Remember that the point of interactive writing is to discuss the message first and then write it. During the writing of the message, the teacher can provide direct instruction about the conventions of language.

Deborah is a fourth-grade student who has been identified as significantly below grade level. While she doesn't seem interested in reading and writing, she is interested in people and what they do. Deborah's teacher, Mr. Foster, uses interactive writing to engage her in literacy instruction. He has selected the "Lives of" series by Kathleen Krull to use with Deborah for several reasons. First, these books provide short biographies of interesting people. Second, the biographies aren't boring: They include bits of gossip and interesting facts about people. And third, the illustrations make the biographies come alive.

Mr. Foster has just finished reading aloud the section on Jack London from *Lives of the Writers* to Deborah. As they discuss the life of this writer, they laugh about the crazy things London did, like asking his guests to swallow goldfish or to put peanuts up their noses.

Mr. Foster comments, "Maybe that's something you'd like to write about. What would you say about Jack London?"

"How about ... Mr. London made great books but teased his friends by doing tricks on them," offers Deborah.

"Did Mr. London make the books?" he asks.

Deborah answers with a smile, "No, he wrote them."

Mr. Foster prompts her to make a meaningful statement, "How would you describe the kinds of tricks he played on his friends?"

"They were crazy! He played crazy tricks on his friends," she giggles.

Through this exchange, they arrive at a new sentence: *Mr. London wrote great books but teased his friends with crazy tricks.* At this point, the writing begins. After Deborah writes each word, she and Mr. Foster recite

> Mr. London wrote great books but teased his friends with crazy tricks

the entire sentence. Once she's finished writing the sentence about Jack London, Mr. Foster follows up by asking Deborah to reread some of her previous sentences. She reads sentences based on different "Lives of . . ." books including selections about Edgar Allan Poe, Cleopatra, and Mozart.

Over time, and with Mr. Foster's investment in her writing, Deborah will learn to craft sentences that convey her ideas accurately. Interactive writing is one way that Mr. Foster is helping Deborah understand that her ideas can be written down so that others can read them.

Background on Research

The development of interactive writing has been greatly influenced by the work of two leading researchers in education—Lev Vygotsky and Marie Clay. Vygotsky's theory of a Zone of Proximal Development (ZPD) (1962) has much to do with the instructional underpinnings of interactive writing. ZPD suggests that learning occurs when a more knowledgeable other interacts with the learner in specific ways. In 1978, Vygotsky described ZPD as the difference between what a child can do with help and what he or she can do without help and that by following the teacher's example, the student gradually learns. The interactive writing process allows students to extend just beyond what they already know about writing because the teacher is there to provide them with support only as it is needed.

The developmental approach to literacy that is characteristic of interactive writing also owes much to the work of Marie Clay. She describes a model of interactive writing that follows "from ideas, to spoken words, to printed messages" (2001). Interactive writing has historically been used with emergent writers (Callella & Jordano, 2002; McCarrier, Pinnell, & Fountas, 2000).

In addition to Vygotsky and Clay, interactive writing draws on the work of other important researchers. As noted by Button, Johnson, and Furgerson (1996), the strategy draws on the instructional practices of both Language Experience Approach (see previous chapter) and shared writing (e.g., Ashton-Warner, 1963; McKenzie, 1985). Shared writing allows teachers and students to construct texts together. The writing is typically based on a book that the class has read, an experience the class has had, or a theme or topic that the class is studying.

As Button, Johnson, and Furgerson (1996) explain in their study of interactive writing, the usefulness of this approach lies in the opportunities for the teacher to focus on a range of skills, including, "conventions of print such as spaces between words, left-to-right and top-to-bottom directionality, capital letters, and punctuation." In addition, our own research with adolescent writers indicates that teachers can focus on phonics, phonemic awareness, spelling, vocabulary, and comprehension (Fisher & Frey, 2003).

Interactive writing has been used to teach English language learners (Fisher & Frey, 2002), to integrate writing and social studies (Button & Welton, 1997), and to develop students' understandings about print (Pinnell & McCarrier, 1994).

KEY POINTS
FOR THE INTERACTIVE WRITING LESSON

Interactive writing is based on the trust that teachers and students have built for one another. In addition, interactive writing requires that students have some understanding of the speech-to-print connections, that they can use this knowledge in their writing, and that they have some experience with writing. To be effective, the interactive writing lesson should include the following:

- *conversation topics based on books or other texts connected to the lesson or a shared experience*

- *conversations to create a consensus, to establish a purpose for writing, and to determine the format of the message*

- *individual students writing sections of the agreed-upon text message*

- *student engagement in extension activities in which they use the interactive writing text*

Building Fluency Through Power Writing

OBJECTIVE: To build writing fluency

ACTIVITY: Students participate in quick, daily timed writing practice, which is repeated three times.

LEVEL OF SUPPORT: Moderate

INSTRUCTIONAL FORMAT: Whole class, small groups, or individual students

Power Writing is a daily fluency activity that requires students to write as many words as well and as fast as they can on a topic. Writing fluency is an important part of the gradual-release framework because it echoes the research on writing sentence parts. In the introduction, we discussed how expert writers construct longer strings of sentence parts before pausing than less-skilled writers do. Writing fluency exercises encourage writers to get their thoughts down on paper quickly.

Power Writing also generates self-created material for students to revise. The goal here is to increase writing fluency so students will build their stamina for writing and also produce work to edit later. Although speed is important in this technique, writing quality is, too. If students concentrate on writing speed at the expense of quality, the revision process may be that much more difficult for them.

Besides building fluency and creating material to revise later, Power Writing requires students to begin writing immediately. This daily procedure pushes writers to avoid stalling and start-and-stop jotting that many of us encounter when we sit down to write.

Features of Power Writing

Implementation: Power Writing is significantly student-controlled. The teacher simply provides a topic or a choice of topics based on prior classroom activities. These may be delivered at the word, phrase, or sentence level. For instance, students may be prompted:

- *Use the word calendar in your Power Write.*

- *Start your Power Write with the phrase, "Once upon a time . . ."*

- *Do you prefer writing with a pen or a pencil? Why?*

A typical Power Writing lesson begins with the teacher asking students to get their writing journals and instruments ready. He or she then sets a timer and instructs students to "write as much as you can as well as you can." Typically, students are given one minute to write. When the timer rings, the teacher says, "Count the number of words you wrote. Then, circle any words you think you may have misspelled and any grammatical errors."

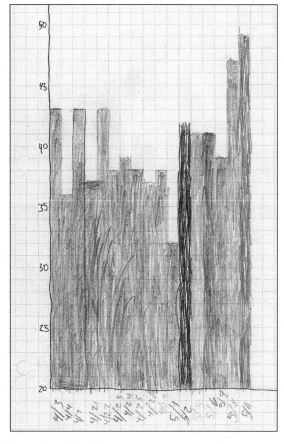

This activity is repeated two more times in succession recording the number of words they've written correctly at the top of each cycle. After the third cycle, students record their best result on a graph in their writer's notebook. Almost everyone will discover that they wrote more words the third time than they did on their first attempt, which is a sure sign of fluency building. The graph serves as an incentive for students, and it allows them to gauge their growing proficiency as fluent writers.

As students become increasingly proficient, teachers vary the amount of writing time from 30 seconds to two minutes or more. The amount of time varies randomly, for instance, from 30 seconds to 120 seconds to 60 seconds so students won't become accustomed to or anticipate writing for a set length of time. They do need to build stamina to write for increasingly longer periods, but we don't want them to focus on the timer. Regardless of the amount of writing time for the prompt, students record their performance in one-minute increments. Thus, if a teacher gives a 30-second prompt, students double their number of words to determine their success rate.

TIP
Statement Goals

Meet with individual students to help them think about and set a reasonable goal for themselves. A teacher-student conversation might sound something like this:

Teacher: Your graph shows that you're writing an average of about twenty words per minute. You might be about to increase this by five words over the next three weeks. Does it sound reasonable for you to try to write twenty-five words per minute?

Student: I think so. I've already written that much a couple of times before.

Teacher: That's true—and your graph shows how much faster you've gotten since we've started doing Power Writing.

When a student meets a goal, schedule another conference to set up a new one. These individual conferences keep students focused on their writing fluency. We suggest meeting at six-week intervals.

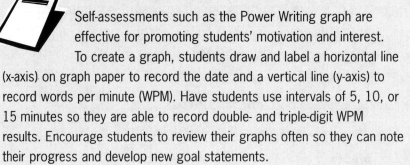

ASSESSMENT LINK

Self-assessments such as the Power Writing graph are effective for promoting students' motivation and interest.

To create a graph, students draw and label a horizontal line (x-axis) on graph paper to record the date and a vertical line (y-axis) to record words per minute (WPM). Have students use intervals of 5, 10, or 15 minutes so they are able to record double- and triple-digit WPM results. Encourage students to review their graphs often so they can note their progress and develop new goal statements.

Students write goals for themselves, indicating how many words they would like to be able to write consistently. Self-efficacy is important. Setting goals for ourselves is motivating and authentic. Personal goals also help the teacher understand the limitations that a student places on himself or herself. We typically ask students to write goal statements after a few weeks of Power Writing practice, and they use their prior performances to set a reasonable goal. These goal statements should contain an expected date, for example: By November 1, I'd like to write at least 40 words per minute.

→ INCREASING METACOGNITIVE AWARENESS

Sometimes, no matter how reasonable a goal seems, a student won't be able to achieve it. Students often say to us that their mind wanders or is blank. They also mention that they couldn't get started right away because they didn't have their materials ready. Others may not be aware of why they are getting stuck as they process their ideas and attempt to put them down on paper. In your individual conversations with students, focus on how they prepare for writing and at what point in the process they get stuck—many students may not even be aware of how they think and act until they discuss it with you. Once you've identified areas of challenge, you can then help students devise techniques for getting started and "unstuck" in their writing. For example, a student may find writing a word over and over until the ideas begin to flow again very helpful. Some accomplished writers may use a form of analogy or simile to get going, such as writing: *(target word) is like a _____ because. . .*

For some students, disfluent writing can be the product of a general lack of metacognitive awareness about the processes writers use. Mubarak, a sixth-grade student from Somalia, is one such student. He often wrote fewer

POWER WRITING OBSERVATION FORM

Name of student: _____

Date of observation: _____

Task, direction, or prompt given: _____

Time allotted for task: _____ WPM: _____

EFFECTIVE POWER WRITING BEHAVIORS

❑ begins writing immediately

❑ materials are ready

❑ few or no crossed-out words

❑ rarely erases

❑ delays rereading until timer rings

❑ pauses are short and infrequent

INEFFECTIVE POWER WRITING BEHAVIORS

❑ hesitates at beginning

❑ stalls by rearranging materials

❑ frequently crosses out words

❑ frequently erases words

❑ stops to reread what has been written

❑ pauses often, lifts pencil from page

Conference notes:

_____

_____

_____

_____

_____

_____

_____

_____

_____

than five words a minute when his teacher, Mr. Jamison, introduced Power Writing to the class in October. Mr. Jamison had noted in previous observations that much of Mubarak's time was spent drumming his pencil and crossing out the few words he'd written. Mr. Jamison wrote "student is distracted; doesn't appear to know where to start; looks stressed by the task." He conferred with Mubarak about this struggle with Power Writing.

They discussed behaviors that would help Mubarak increase his average words per minute. Mr. Jamison shared his observational notes and explained to Mubarak that he didn't need to reread and edit during these brief writing events. This seemed to come as a surprise to Mubarak, who told Mr. Jamison that he thought the direction "write as well as you can" meant to write very carefully. Mubarak simply needed to understand that Power Writing was a brainstorming activity for getting ideas down quickly and that editing and revision would come later when he chose pieces for further development.

These three samples of Mubarak's Power Writing show the change in his writing output during the year.

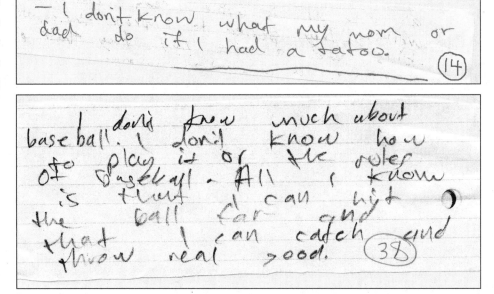

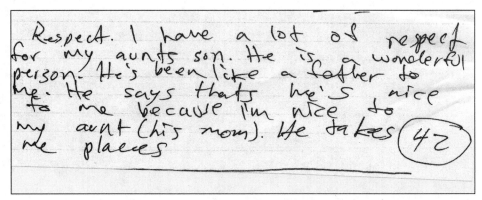

By that March, Mubarak averaged 40 words a minute! Naturally, his papers contained errors, many of which were common errors that English language learners often make. Mr. Jamison was able to use these errors to plan instruction for him. In addition, Mubarak was increasingly able to recognize and circle the errors in his own work. This indicated a real growth in reading fluency as well as writing fluency. Just as importantly, the act of writing every day for a defined period of time allowed Mubarak to understand and achieve the flow that more accomplished writers experience.

FOLLOW-UP ACTIVITIES

As with other pieces of writing, you may want students to use their Power Writing responses for follow-up writing activities. For example, you can ask them to do the following:

- *revise their writing and produce a polished draft*
- *peer edit and discuss recommended changes*
- *write found poems*

Using Power Writing With the Whole Class

Ms. Allen uses Power Writing in her fifth-grade classroom on a daily basis, and her students write on three topics every day. As you'll see, Ms. Allen makes Power Writing quite a production.

Ms. Allen: Pencils up!
(Students open their journals and hold their pencils in the air.)

Ms. Allen: We've been reading and discussing books about people who make a difference as part of our daily shared reading and in our literature circles. The idea of celebrations has come up in some of our conversations. Today, I'd like you to write as much as you can, as well as you can, about celebrations.
(She sets the timer for one minute, and students immediately begin writing.)

The other two topics in Ms. Allen's class that day were *pride* and *honor*. The next day, she asked her students to write on the topics *life*, *liberty*, and *happiness*. All of these topics had come up in classroom and group conversations about people who make a difference.

The record for Ms. Allen's class is 87 words written in one minute—a rare and significant number. In general, we hope that students can achieve at least 40 words per minute by the time they are in fifth grade. The average in the class at the start of the year was 18 words per minute, with a range of 1 to 28 words. By February, the average had increased to 34 words, with a range of 12 to 87 words! (For more information about how to use these numbers to plan Power Writing instruction in your classroom, refer to Chapter 2 on Assessment.)

FOLLOW-UP ACTIVITIES

The daily Power Writing practice is often followed up by activities that utilize the students' work. Besides writing more words, students appreciate knowing that their writing has an additional purpose. Here are two example activities to use with your whole class.

> My mom
> Walking home
> Talking, talking, talking
> Friends outside
> Talking, talking, talking
> Sisters and brothers inside
> Talking, talking, talking
> They all care about me

Maggie's Found Poem

- *Have students take their Power Writing material to a writing center in order to work with peers to revise one of the selections. (See Chapter 2 for an effective peer feedback model to use with students). To ensure that peers aren't simply providing "global praise" or only focusing on mechanics errors, you may want to collect and review student drafts, peer feedback sheets, and the final versions.*

- *Encourage students to review their writing and select key words to spur the creation of an open-verse poem "found poem." For example, one of Ms. Allen's students Maggie wrote a found poem based on the Power Writing topic of happiness.*

> Happiness is walking home with my mom. We spend it talking, talking, talking. I see my friends outside. All my sisters and brothers are inside the house. My mom and I are still talking. I'm happy because they all care about me.

Maggie's Power Writing

Using Power Writing With Small Groups

Students also may be assigned to Power Writing groups consisting of four to six students. Each group is a heterogeneous mix of stronger and emerging writers. The groups meet daily at a learning center to complete their Power Writing practice. Each group member takes turns drawing a topic from a jar of possible ideas. (The teacher adds topics based on the content the class is studying, and students propose additional subjects of interest.) The student reads the idea to the others and then sets the timer for one minute. Everyone writes until the timer goes off. As with all Power Writing activities, this writing activity is done a total of three times. Each student then graphs his or her highest number of written words. One week, Ms. Allen filled the jar with these Power Writing prompts:

- *How are you responsible for your own learning?*
- *Use the word* **perimeter** *in your Power Write.*
- *Start the first sentence with the word* **Earth.**
- *San Diego Chargers*
- *What were you like in first grade?*
- *Use the word* **strength** *in your Power Write.*
- *Use the phrase "I'm smart" in your Power Write.*
- *What kind of food are you really good at making?*
- *Start with the words "Music is. . ."*
- *Sandy beach*
- *Do you like rainy days?*

At the end of the day, as a follow-up activity, the teacher can randomly select a group to take their Power Writing home, edit it, and bring it back to class the following day. These edited pieces are then reviewed by members of their group, rewritten as needed by the author, and submitted to the teacher.

Groups follow this procedure in Ms. Allen's classroom for a variety of reasons. First, it would be impossible for her to read thirty papers every day. However, reading four to six papers per day is manageable. In addition, students are more likely to take the Power Writing activity seriously if they never know when they might be asked to submit an edited version of their work to the teacher.

TIP
Introducing Procedures

It's important to model the procedure for the small-group Power Writing practice in front of the whole class. Show students how the timer works and explain the responsibilities of the group leader for choosing and reading the Power Writing topics. Remind students about recording their individual results. Having procedures in place—and making sure that students understand them—helps to ensure that groups will be able to complete their tasks.

Using Power Writing With Individual Students

Power Writing is effective with groups of students, and most teachers use it in that format. However, Power Writing also can be used with individual students to help them focus on what they think about a specific topic.

Mr. Anderson meets with individual students several times each week to help them brainstorm ideas for their writing. During these conferences, the other students are engaged in independent reading and writing activities.

When Mr. Anderson meets with Jesse, he often uses Power Writing to focus Jesse on the topic at hand. For example, during their reading of *Charlotte's Web* by E. B. White, Mr. Anderson stops reading and asks Jesse to write as much as he can as fast as he can about the importance of a special place. Mr. Anderson starts the timer for one minute, and Jesse begins writing. After the timer rings, Jesse counts his words and then writes the total at the bottom of the page.

Then they have a conversation comparing Wilbur's comments and Jesse's thoughts about the importance of having a special place. Part of their conversation appears below:

Mr. Anderson: How many words did you write that time?

Jesse: Eighteen!

Mr. Anderson: Great, that's more than you wrote last time, isn't it?

Jesse: Yeah, last time I only did fourteen words.

Mr. Anderson: Tell me about the special place you wrote about.

Jesse: I wrote about the soccer field.

Mr. Anderson: What makes it so special for you?

Jesse: It kind of makes me feel safe, like Wilbur feels.

Mr. Anderson: Can you tell me more about how it makes you feel safe?

Jesse: You know, like I feel like I'm good there. Like I won't get things wrong.

Mr. Anderson: Do you feel like you get a lot of things wrong?

Jesse: Yeah . . . sometimes, I rush around too much, and I make mistakes.

Mr. Anderson: I'm glad you have a special place where you feel good. Let's talk more about it. Describe the soccer field to me, and I'll take some notes about it.

Jesse: Well ... it's green.

Mr. Anderson: Good. Go on.

Jesse: I mean, it's green and open, and there are lines and lots of people. They're all yelling—but good yelling.

Mr. Anderson: What else?

Jesse: And eating—my mom always gets something to eat when I'm playing soccer.

Mr. Anderson: Look at all the notes I've taken. I wrote down all of your great ideas about your special place. Can you take my notes and your eighteen words and revise them during your independent writing time?

Jesse: Yeah, I think so.

Mr. Anderson: Good, let's meet day after tomorrow to talk about what you've written. Then we'll have you do a peer-review conference, and I'll give you some feedback, too. Does that sound like a plan?

Power Writing and the associated follow-up activities are an important component of teaching students to write well. The Power Writing drafts offer the opportunity to revise and edit. Similarly, the impetus for peer-review conferences and teacher-conferring sessions is existing student writing. Power Writing ensures that students have thought about topics and written about them.

Background on Research

Experts agree that fluency in reading is critical to comprehension (LaBerge & Samuels, 1974; Rasinski, 2003). Unfortunately, the role of writing fluency in writing skill development or achievement has received significantly less attention. We do, however, have some understanding of what writing fluency looks like and why it is critical to effective writing. Hayes and Flower (1980) describe a three-fold writing process that experienced writers use: planning the writing, translating the plans onto the page, and reviewing what has been written. Many struggling writers struggle with the first two parts of this process, thus allowing themselves fewer opportunities to engage in the third. Peter Elbow (1981) developed the strategy of freewriting as a way to jump-start the process and overcome the "writer's block" that plagues many students. He suggested that many writers attempt to write and edit simultaneously, and that this habit can be paralyzing. Elbow found that freewriting exercises helped writers break these interfering behaviors.

While the research on writing fluency has been limited, it is promising. For example, Kasper-Ferguson and Moxley (2002) focused on fourth-grade students' writing fluency and demonstrated that, in addition to being able to write more words per minute, the quality of their writing also increased. Via daily writing prompts and the graphing of these results, students demonstrated more sophisticated organization and greater use of details. Interestingly, over the year, there was no ceiling effect: Writing fluency was still increasing at the end of the year and had not yet topped out.

Similarly Moxley, Lutz, Ahborn, Boley, and Armstrong (1995) evaluated the use of self-recorded word counts of loose and restricted-time freewriting in grades 1, 2, 3, and 4. In each case, the number of words written in a

NO MORE UNIFORMS ♀♀♀

Our school wears uniforms and they are really ugly. If we could wear what we want. I think it would be much better. Kids might even like to come to school more often. Even though we go to school to learn, we still want to look good at the same time.

The reason why uniforms are ugly is because they come in only certin colors and are plain. You cant even wear what you want without getting in trouble. Uniform are really the most hated things at school. H_____ inks they are expensive, b_____ just a waste of _____ clothes are probably _____ we could wear those _____ ne, there is nothing _____ orms. Plus, uniforms _____ even my grandma wouldn't _____ them.

Regular clothes are really good because they are in style and alot of kids like to wear them. I think if the kids at our school would complain less if we got to wear whatever we want. My mom and dad think things would change around the school if we could wear the clothes we want. Regular clothes are much more comfortable to wear. Wearing something that is itchy can bug you and it would be very uncomfortable.

We wear uniforms at school and they are so ugly. None even wants to come to school. We want to look good!

session increased over time, and this increase accompanied improvements in expressiveness. These researchers also noted that "Increases in writing rates were also accompanied by increases in concrete detail, such as dialogue, and in sentence complexity, as indicated by both word length and syntax."

In grades 6 through 8, Fisher, Frey, Fearn, Farnan, and Petersen (2004) noted that writing achievement was significantly improved when the entire school focused on writing, when teachers scored common writing prompts, and when students engaged in timed writing activities.

KEY POINTS
ABOUT USING POWER WRITING

Power Writing is a brief instructional task that focuses students on writing fluency. Over time, they develop the ability to write more. This provides them with fodder for revision and refinement. Power Writing also allows students literally to see what they think. To be effective, the Power Writing lesson should include the following:

- *three one-minute timed writing cycles*
- *a cue encouraging students to "write as much as they can, as well as they can"*
- *time for students to reread their writing and circle or underline errors*
- *the opportunity for students to graph their progress*

Generative Writing

OBJECTIVE: To compose written messages based on given words

ACTIVITY: Given specific parameters, students use their understanding of syntax and sentence structure to construct meaningful texts.

LEVEL OF SUPPORT: Modest

INSTRUCTIONAL FORMAT: Use with whole class, small groups, or individual students

Generative writing is a term used to describe instructional strategies that provide students with parameters for their writing. These factors define boundaries for writing at the sentence and paragraph levels.

At the sentence level:

- *providing a word to be used*
- *defining the word's position in the sentence*
- *specifying the number of words in the sentence*
- *limiting the number of words in a sentence*
- *stating the sentence pattern (syntax)*

At the paragraph level:

- *sentence combining*

We use generative writing as craft exercises for powerful expression. Students who write well at the sentence and paragraph levels are likely to do so in longer pieces. The reverse is unlikely—if you can't write sentences and paragraphs well, you most likely can't write longer pieces well either.

Generative writing also supports students' growing fluency. Because these pieces are short and students begin their composition at the word, or even the letter level, they encourage students to delve into concentrated writing of short texts—and improve their structure and syntax. Consider this sequence:

1. Think of a word that begins with the letter *b*. Write down that word.
2. Use that word in the second position of a sentence.
3. Use this sentence as the first line in a paragraph.

In three steps, you've moved from a letter of the alphabet to a paragraph. This is helpful for the students who hem and haw, waiting for inspiration to visit them. Generative writing represents a shift from Power Writing, where the idea is to get words on paper. With generative writing, the ante is upped a bit as boundaries are established. The instructional strategies in this chapter allow for specific instruction in sentence grammar, word choice, and style.

Every teacher knows that students often make mistakes at the sentence level. Generative writing allows students to create sentences that are increasingly sophisticated. It also provides them with a way to expand their sentences and to be able to use the language and mechanics necessary to convey information. Further, generative writing helps teachers assess whether or not students can produce meaningful units that are grammatically correct.

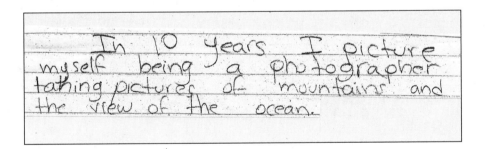

Keep in mind that establishing parameters for writing should not be confused with formula writing. Frankly, we're not enamored of the widespread approach to writing instruction that encourages students to "fill in the blanks" through sentence starters and hamburger paragraphs. These are contrived and limit the voice of young writers by wedging them into a box that no one else uses outside of school. When was the last time you read a hamburger paragraph on the editorial page of your favorite newspaper?

TIP
Using Student Samples
Use generative writing to focus whole-class discussions on the craft of writing; rather than relying on daily oral language activities to work on correcting errors, share samples of students' writing (with their names removed). These samples can be placed on the overhead projector and used to illustrate writing mechanics and craft.

Mariah, a fifth-grade student, wrote this sentence when her teacher asked students to generate a sentence using the word **photographer.** *Her sentence became the prompt for a much longer piece of writing.*

Features of Generative Writing at the Sentence Level

Implementation: To begin the generative sentence session, the teacher selects several words and considers how he or she will ask students to construct a sentence with the word. For example, he or she may choose words that have been introduced during a specific unit of study, such as *body*, *heart*, and *lungs*.

- *Use the word* body *in the second position in the sentence.* *(generative sentence)*

- *Use the word* heart *in a sentence of at least seven words.* *(word limiting)*

- *Use the word* lungs *in a sentence with a prepositional phrase. (sentence pattern)*

Each of these types of prompts is increasingly more challenging, and each provides the teacher with an opportunity to discuss craft.

GENERATIVE SENTENCES: Once the words are selected, the teacher must determine the placement of the word in the sentence—first word, third word, last word, or any other position. Students are then asked to write a sentence using the word in the specific place. In addition to writing skills, these exercises provide assessment information about content knowledge.

For instance, sixth-grade students produced the following sentences:

- *Her <u>body</u> was broken like a car that just won't start.*

- *My <u>body</u> is in great shape.*

- *Your <u>body</u> needs nutrients, protein, and water to survive.*

The writer of the third sentence seems to have integrated science content into her sentence, while the others have not.

ASSESSMENT LINK

Alternatively, the selected words may allow the teacher to assess and then target an area of grammar or syntax in which students need instruction, such as when to use the homophones *they're*, *there*, and *their* or how to begin a sentence with the word *because*.

WORD LIMITING: The teacher may also set a limit on the total number of words in the sentence, for instance, an upper limit (e.g., a sentence with no more than eight words) or a lower limit (e.g., in a sentence with at least ten words). The sixth-grade students mentioned previously wrote the following for their second generative sentence:

- My <u>heart</u> was broken at camp last summer.

- Older people need to eat right or they can have a <u>heart</u> attack.

- The <u>heart</u> has four chambers and pumps blood.

A word limiter challenges students to mentally manipulate language to meet the criterion. While arbitrary, it's a useful exercise for discussions about style at the paragraph and text level, since accomplished writers vary the length of sentences to create interest. Generative sentences that limit the overall length cause young writers to be succinct and not go on and on, adding needless phrases just to make a longer sentence (like this one).

ASSESSMENT LINK

Display student examples of generative sentences on the overhead or write them on the board, and discuss their features. Authentic student writing provides great examples for highlighting variations. Student errors serve as teachable moments for improving the skills of all students. Be sure to keep the writing anonymous or to ask students' permission to display their work.

SENTENCE PATTERNING: A third type of generative sentence requires the use of a defined pattern such as including a part of speech, punctuation, or element of style. The sixth graders wrote their third generative sentence using prepositional phrases relating to the subject *lungs*:

- <u>Of all the organs,</u> your lungs are very important.

- The lungs <u>in your chest</u> move the air in and out.

- Your lungs are <u>in front</u> of your heart.

A list of prompts for generative sentences appears on page 94.

LETTER PLACING	Word that begins with _____ . Word that contains _____ . Word that contains _____ in the _____ position.
GENERATIVE SENTENCES	Begin a sentence with _____ . End a sentence with _____ . Create a sentence with _____ in the _____ position.
WORD LIMITING	Provide a range (e.g., eight to ten words in length) Provide a minimum (e.g., at least five words in length) Provide a maximum (e.g., no more that 11 words in length) Provide a specific length (e.g., exactly eight words in length)
SENTENCE PATTERNING: **Parts of Speech**	Begin a sentence with a noun. Use a proper noun in a sentence. Use a noun and a pronoun in a sentence. Include an adjective with the target word. Use an adverb in the third position in the sentence. Include a preposition in your sentence. Use _____ as a gerund. Use a noun infinitive to make an interesting sentence.
SENTENCE PATTERNING: **Punctuation**	Write a sentence that ends an exclamation mark. Ask a question using the word _____ . Write a sentence with an independent clause and a semicolon. Use a colon with a list. Include a parenthetical expression in a sentence.
SENTENCE PATTERNING: **Elements of Style**	Write an imperative using the word _____ . Create a sentence with a prepositional phrase. Use a possessive with the target word _____ . Begin a sentence with a dependent clause. Write a sentence that uses alliteration. Use _____ as a simile. Include an appositive in a sentence with the word _____ .

In a typical generative sentences lesson, a teacher assigns three to five words, and students write a sentence for each. Once the students have written their sentences, they are ready for extended activities such as word pyramids and syntax surgery, described below.

✔ FOLLOW-UP ACTIVITIES FOR GENERATIVE SENTENCES

• Syntax surgery, developed by Adrienne Herrell, allows students to see and correct the grammatical errors they make in their generative sentences. This is especially important for English language learners who confuse word order when they speak, read, and write English. The syntax surgery process involves writing the sentence on a strip of paper, cutting apart the words, and reassembling the sentence in the correct order using the conventions of English.

• Word pyramids are useful for expanding students' writing vocabularies. Students are given a theme or topic and asked to generate a list of related words. The words are written pyramid-style, beginning with a two-letter word and expanding by one additional letter in length until the student cannot generate any more words. These words are then used to write sentences featuring each of the words. A seventh-grade student who was asked to create a word pyramid using the letter *N* wrote the following:

TIP

Reference Materials

Keep dictionaries and thesauri on hand when using word pyramids. Students will find these reference materials useful in developing semantically related words, or those beginning with a common letter. Remind your students that they will be generating sentences using these words, so they should choose wisely.

N -
No - No One is going to School today.
Not - Not everyOne is Heading to the Diners.
Noun - The girl does not know Her Nouns.
Nymph - The Nymph Hid in the Forest.
Nibble - The Mouse Nibbled on the Cheese.
Nuclear - The Nuclear Bomb Destroyed everything.
Nintendo - The Nintendo Broke
Nocturnal - The Owl is an Nocturnal creature.
narcissim - They Hate people with narcissism.

Features of Generative Writing at the Paragraph Level

Generative writing can extend to the paragraph level through the use of sentence combining. Skillful sentence combining is an important skill that good writers use to vary sentence length and increase the reader's interest while reducing unnecessary verbiage. Students are taught to combine short sentences by using conjunctions, phrase modifiers, or compound verbs and subjects to make complex sentences. For example, the following sentences can be improved through combining:

Some sentences are short. Some sentences are choppy. These can be hard to read. Some sentences can be combined. This can be more interesting to read.

Combined: *Some short and choppy sentences can be combined to be more interesting to read.*

Sentence combining can be difficult for students who lack strong syntactical knowledge. Frequent sentence combining sessions for students of all ages and writing abilities can be beneficial, but it needs to be taught throughout the year, not simply as a two-week grammar unit that is never revisited. We have found that the books we read in our classroom are a great source of examples for sentence combining. Simply take a well-written paragraph and rewrite it using choppy and redundant sentences.

ASSESSMENT LINK

Assess the syntactic knowledge of your students by administering a cloze passage. This is a passage with every fifth word removed and replaced with a blank. Students read and fill in the blanks using their knowledge of the content and the syntax of the language. You can create one of your own by using a grade level passage of 50–250 words. Leave the title and the first and last sentences intact, and cover every fifth word. Analyze the results of the assessment by determining the types of errors that students made. Note when the student makes errors related to tense, noun-verb agreements, articles, and other parts of speech. These errors indicate difficulty with grammar and syntax.

Show students how the passage can be improved using sentence combining, and compare their results to the author's original paragraph. The goal is not for students to faithfully duplicate the author's paragraph but rather for you to highlight and discuss the many ways in which writers solve the problem of making their paragraphs more interesting. Use several student examples to show your writers about the options available to them.

Using Generative Writing With the Whole Class: Sentence Combining

The students in Ms. Wilson's seventh-grade class have been reading about Phineas Gage in their science textbook, and she has decided to use their interest in the topic to practice sentence combining. They have read about the plight of Phineas in their study of brain science, so Ms. Wilson writes a paragraph on his injury to model the ways in which writers make decisions about the continuity and clarity of a paragraph. She writes each sentence on a long strip of paper and places them in a pocket chart:

- *Phineas Gage was a railroad worker who suffered a terrible accident.*
- *It happened in 1848.*
- *Phineas Gage is probably the most famous patient to have survived severe damage to the brain.*
- *He is also the first patient from whom we learned something about the relation between personality and the function of the front parts of the brain.*
- *An explosion blew a tamping rod through his head.*
- *Although he survived the accident, he was never the same.*
- *He was a kind and responsible man before the accident.*
- *He was unreliable and untrustworthy after the accident.*
- *He died in 1860.*

Ms. Wilson introduces the activity and explains that her goal is to reduce the overall number of sentences from nine to six. She reads aloud her paragraph, pointing out how uneven it sounds. Then she returns to the first two sentences.

"Listen to this: *Phineas Gage was a railroad worker who suffered a terrible accident. It happened in 1848.* Yuck! I can cut out *It happened* and combine the two first two sentences. Listen to it now: *Phineas Gage was a railroad worker who suffered a terrible accident in 1848.* That's not too complicated. I decided to make that change because I didn't need those two extra words. *It* refers to the "terrible accident" mentioned in the first sentence. That's a good way for me to make a decision: Look for pronouns to see if I can combine phrases and eliminate unnecessary words."

Ms. Wilson continues to model her choices as she combines sentences, taking time to explain exactly what she has done to the syntax. Soon, she has assembled the following sentences: *Phineas Gage was a railroad worker who suffered a terrible accident in 1848. Although he survived the accident, he was never the same. Kind and responsible before the accident, he was unreliable and untrustworthy after.*

She tells the class, "Now, I've got to keep in mind that I can't lose the meaning while I'm combining sentences. I can change their order, though. I'm going to take the third and fourth sentences on this sheet of paper and move them to the beginning of the paragraph. I've noticed that they sound like topic sentences because they've got some main ideas in them."

Ms. Wilson continues to cut apart words and phrases. With assistance from her students, she develops a new lead sentence by combining the original third and fourth sentences. She places it at the top of the pocket chart:

Phineas Gage is probably the most famous patient to have survived severe damage to the brain, and the first from whom we learned something about the relationship between personality and the function of the front parts of the brain. Phineas Gage was a railroad worker who suffered a terrible accident in 1848. Although he survived the accident, he was never the same. Kind and responsible before the accident, he was unreliable and untrustworthy after.

She comments, "Wow! That's a long sentence! I have to be careful not to string too many long sentences together. I don't want to confuse my readers." She rereads the newly assembled paragraph. "Yes, that works, because my second sentence about Phineas' accident is shorter. I like the change in the rhythm between the two, although I can get rid of the name *Phineas Gage* in that second sentence now. It sounds funny to start two sentences in a row with the same words. I'll replace it with *He.*"

Ms. Wilson continues to model sentence combining until she has reduced the paragraph to six sentences. She then provides students with sentences to create a follow-up paragraph. This time, she gives them a paper copy formatted with single sentences in boxes. Equipped with scissors and glue sticks, student partners combine sentences and attach them to a sheet of paper.

Using Generative Writing With Small Groups: Generative Sentences

Ms. Raafat has identified a group of reluctant writers in her fourth-grade classroom and has called them to her guided writing table to give them some specific instruction on generative sentences. She's identified these students through observation and has noted their difficulty in getting started during short writing exercises. She has also administered a normed writing attitude survey earlier in the year to gauge student beliefs and perceptions about writing. Kimberley, Arthur, and Eddie scored at the 18th, 27th, and 32nd percentile respectively, and Ms. Raafat has been meeting with them twice a week to work on their writing. In particular, she has been concerned about shifting their attitudes about the perceived difficulty of writing. In this lesson, she has decided to use a generative writing exercise to jump-start their compositions:

Ms. Raafat welcomes the group to the writing table and explains that she's going to get them started on a creative writing assignment the class will be doing later in the week. She begins her instruction at the letter level and gradually works toward the word and sentence levels of generative writing.

Ms. Raafat: I'm going to get you writing before you know it! Here's the first step. Everyone write the letter *v* on your paper. When you've done that, think of a word that has the letter *v* in the third position. For instance, I'll write the word *love*. (She pauses while students write.) Now, tell me what you wrote.

Arthur: Have.

Eddie: Dove.

Kimberley: What's that?

Eddie: It's like a bird.

Ms. Raafat: Kimberley, what word did you write?

Kimberley: I wrote give.

Ms. Raafat: Good work! I've got those written down on our list. Let's think of a few more.

In a matter of minutes, the list has grown and includes *love, have, dove, give, advice, live, cave,* and *save.* Ms. Raafat asks them to choose one of the words and use it in the second position in a sentence. She models one for them: *The cave was dark and damp.* Eddie and Kimberley put their heads down to write, but Arthur hesitates.

Ms. Raafat: Arthur, I'll help you. Draw six or seven blank lines on your paper. We'll fill in words. (Arthur does so, then Ms. Raafat continues.) Which word do you want to use? Write that word in the second blank.

Arthur: I got it. Now what?

Ms. Raafat: You wrote *dove.* Can you put a word in front of that?

Arthur: The. The dove.

Ms. Raafat: There you go. Finish that idea. What about the dove?

Arthur: Well, it means peace.

Ms. Raafat: Say a whole idea. The dove…

Arthur: The dove means peace.

Ms. Raafat: Can you make it better?

Arthur: The dove is a sign of peace.

Ms. Raafat: That sounds like a good sentence to me! Write those words in the blanks. (She waits for Arthur to finish.) Now, let's hear all your sentences.

Eddie: I love my family, especially James.

Arthur: The dove is a sign of peace.

Kimberley: My advice is that you best get some advice on that hairdo.

Ms. Raafat laughs at this last sentence and then talks with Kimberley about syntax. Kimberley changes the sentence: *My advice is to get some advice on that hairdo.* Next, she asks the students to use their sentence as a topic sentence for a paragraph. She reminds them that a paragraph doesn't have a fixed number of sentences, and it could be three, five, eight—whatever number of sentences is necessary to convey the idea they want to share.

Ms. Raafat: Write your paragraph for homework tonight, and we'll confer about them tomorrow to see how it can be used for your creative writing assignment. I like the way you got your ideas down on paper today. Sometimes writers have to break it down into small parts to get themselves going.

Consistent with the gradual-release model, Ms. Raafat's teaching helps her struggling writers create a topic sentence in class and begin to complete the paragraph assigned for homework. Ms. Raafat has found that the completion rate of this scaffolded homework writing assignment is much higher for these students than independent writing assignments in which they must complete an entire paper at home.

ASSESSMENT LINK

We introduced the Writing Attitude Survey (WAS) (Kear, Coffman, McKenna, & Ambrosio, 2000) in Chapter 2. The survey is a normed survey for students in grades 1 through 12. The survey can be group-administered and takes about 20 minutes. It consists of 28 items, such as: *How would you feel if you didn't write as much in school?* Participants respond by circling one of four Garfield cartoon characters in various states of emotion from overjoyed to angry. The raw scores are converted into percentile scores for each grade level. The WAS is available at no cost from the International Reading Association and can be duplicated for classroom use. Contact:

International Reading Association
800 Barksdale Road
P.O. Box 8139
Newark, DE 19714-8139

Using Generative Writing With Individual Students: Syntax Surgery

While syntax surgery is useful for all students, many teachers use this strategy with individual English language learners to reinforce the rules of grammar. For example, third-grade teacher Mr. Caldera meets with Katerina, a girl originally from the Czech Republic who is learning English. He has assessed her using the Student Oral Language Observation Matrix (SOLOM), an observational instrument that allows teachers to rate a student's proficiency in English (see page 103). While the instrument invites consideration of dimensions of oral language such as comprehension, fluency, vocabulary, and pronunciation, Mr. Caldera has found it to be useful for writing instruction as well. He gave Katerina a rating of two (out of five) on grammar, meaning that he had observed her making word order errors that interfered with comprehension. He has decided to use Syntax Surgery as part of his individual instruction to expand Katerina's literacy skills in English.

ASSESSMENT LINK

Oral language assessments, such as the SOLOM assessment, can provide insight into the way a child uses and understands language. While not direct assessments of writing ability, they can give you important information about students' control of syntactic elements.

Mr. Caldera asks Katerina to write a sentence with the word *green* in it. He tells her that the word *green* can be in any place in the sentence but that the sentence must be at least six words long. Katerina writes: *Green it is the color of the tree.* Mr. Caldera congratulates her on the sentence and copies it onto a sentence strip. He then cuts it apart, word by word, to reassemble. An excerpt from the lesson follows:

Mr. Caldera: Let's see what we can do with that sentence. Katerina, let's put the words back together the way you wrote it, and then I'll read it aloud.

Katerina: Like this?

Mr. Caldera: Yes, exactly. Now listen to the sentence. *Green it is the color of the tree.* I'm noticing an extra word in there that the sentence doesn't need.

Katerina: Which one?

Mr. Caldera: There's a pronoun that the sentence doesn't need. Remember our work with pronouns? You and I have been working with *he, she,* and *it.* Those are words that take the place of a person, place, or thing. Find the thing—the *it* in your sentence.

Katerina: Is it *tree*?

Mr. Caldera: Let's read it again. *Green it is the color of the tree.* I know that the pronoun takes the place of a thing that came earlier in the sentence. Is *tree* before or after it?

SOLOM (STUDENT ORAL LANGUAGE OBSERVATION MATRIX)

Student's Name _____ Grade _____ Language Observed _____ Date _____

	A. Comprehension	B. Fluency	C. Vocabulary	D. Pronunciation	E. Grammar
1	Cannot be said to understand even simple conversation.	Speech is so halting and fragmentary as to make conversation virtually impossible.	Vocabulary limitations so extreme as to make conversation virtually impossible.	Pronunciation problems so severe as to make speech virtually impossible.	Errors in grammar and word order so severe as to make speech virtually unintelligible.
2	Has great difficulty following what is said. Can comprehend only "social conversation" spoken slowly and with frequent repetitions.	Usually hesitant; often forced into silence by language limitations.	Misuse of words and very limited vocabulary make comprehension quite difficult.	Very hard to understand because of pronunciation problems. Must frequently repeat in order to make himself/herself understood.	Grammar and word order errors make comprehension difficult. Must often rephrase and/or restrict himself/herself to basic patterns.
3	Understands most of what is said at slower-than normal speed with repetitions.	Speech in everyday conversation and classroom discussion is frequently disrupted by the student's search for the correct manner of expression.	Frequently uses the wrong words; conversation somewhat limited because of inadequate vocabulary.	Pronunciation problems necessitate concentration on the part of the listener and occasionally lead to misunderstanding.	Makes frequent errors of grammar and word order, which occasionally obscure meaning.
4	Understands nearly everything at normal speech, although occasional repetition may be necessary.	Speech in everyday conversation and classroom discussions is generally fluent, with occasional lapses while the student searches for the correct manner of expression.	Occasionally uses inappropriate terms and/or must rephrase ideas because of lexical inadequacies.	Always intelligible, though one is conscious of a definite accent and occasional inappropriate patterns.	Occasionally makes grammatical and/or word-order errors which do not obscure meaning.
5	Understands everyday conversation and normal classroom discussions without difficulty.	Speech in everyday conversation and classroom discussions is fluent and effortless approximating that of a native speaker.	Use of vocabulary and idioms approximates that of a native speaker.	Pronunciation and intonation approximates that of a native speaker.	Grammatical usage and word order approximates that of a native speaker.

Katerina: After. After it.

Mr. Caldera: There you go! What thing comes before *it*?

Katerina: *Green.* (She slides the word card to Mr. Caldera.)

Mr. Caldera: Now you've got it. Our sentence has *green* and *it* right next to each other, so I know I don't need one of those words. Let's get rid of *green* and see if that works. (He removes that card.) *It is the color of the tree.* Does that sentence make sense?

Katerina: Yes, it makes sense.

Mr. Caldera: But what is *it*? What is the color of the tree?

Katerina: (giggling) Green, Mr. Caldera! Trees are green!

Mr. Caldera: I could make the sentence better by using *green* instead of *it*. Let's switch the word cards and read it again. *Green is the color of the tree.* What do you think of our sentence now?

Katerina: It's better. Can I write it?

Mr. Caldera: Yes, write it down, and then let's write another sentence. This time we'll use *it* to talk about the color green.

Mr. Caldera and Katerina construct a second sentence, discussing how to use the pronoun as a referent to the word *green*. Together, they write: *It is the color of a frog.* Katerina will need many lessons on syntax, but this activity has proven useful for letting her manipulate the order of words without the frustration children often feel when they fix errors in their writing.

Background on Research

Our work with generative sentences builds on Fearn and Farnan's "Given Word Sentences" (2001). In particular, we use generative writing as a stepping stone to more sophisticated writing, especially as students develop paragraphs to extend the ideas first discovered through exercises.

Generative Writing can be used to scaffold for students increasingly challenging problems in structure and syntax. Dorn and Soffos (2001) point out that there is a continuum of difficulty even within generative writing:

- Adding words (the easiest)
- Deleting words
- Substituting words
- Rearranging sentences (the most difficult)

Time spent on the construction of sentences has proven to be a sound investment for young writers. For instance, kindergartners are still figuring out the relationships between words in a sentence at the syntactic and semantic levels. They have more difficulty with sentences that contain many functor words such as *with*, *of*, and *by* (Manning, Manning, & Long, 1995). Work with generative sentences allows for conversation and instruction about this syntax.

Research shows that sentence combining helps students organize their writing. Mellon (1969) and O'Hare (1973) were among the first to describe sentence combining instruction. The effectiveness of this strategy seems to come from the opportunity to teach about grammar and syntax within context. Saddler and Graham (2005) found that fourth graders who were taught sentence combining outperformed similarly achieving students who were given traditional grammar instruction. Interestingly, in a study of fifth graders, McAfee (1980) noted that students who were taught to combine sentences scored significantly better than a control group in both reading comprehension and written expression. Further, the data from this study indicated that students who received sentence combining instruction demonstrated significant gains in their writing achievement compared with students who did not receive this type of instruction. Similarly, Enginarlar (1994) demonstrated the use of sentence combining as an effective instructional strategy for English language learners.

KEY POINTS
FOR THE USE OF GENERATIVE WRITING

To become effective writers, students must learn how to create powerful and engaging sentences. This requires knowledge of words and how they can be combined in novel ways to produce messages that grab the reader. It also requires the ability to vary sentence length and to be concise and efficient in writing. Students are taught to think about and practice sentence manipulation in generative sentence activities. In addition, the errors in grammar and structure students make as they generate sentences provides rich material for future instruction.

There are two important things to remember when using generative sentences. The first is that the word chosen must work in the sentence in the position requested. In other words, the task must be doable and should result in the assessment information you want. Second, simply generating sentences is not enough. The sentences need to be reviewed and revised. You'll want to use the results from these generative sentences to plan focus lessons in which specific components of language are taught (Frey & Fisher, 2006; Parkes, 2000).

To be effective, the generative writing lesson should include the following:

- a definition of parameters for word usage, count, or position so students have to consider both the syntactic and semantic features of the sentence

- a model sentence or paragraph that works given these parameters

- a time for teachers and students to review results so that follow-up instruction can be planned

Writing Models

OBJECTIVE: To construct new texts using models of good writing

ACTIVITY: Students use mentor texts to create their own writing.

LEVEL OF SUPPORT: Limited

INSTRUCTIONAL FORMAT: Use with whole class, small groups, or individual students

Have you ever completed or assigned an acrostic or other alphabet poem? Perhaps you've asked your students to write a poem about Native Americans, with the first letter of each line spelling out the word *Iroquois*. Or you asked them to use the alphabet to list words that describe the animals and plants of the Amazon rain forest. It's possible you've taught using shape poems or story pyramids. These are perhaps the most obvious examples of writing models.

Writing models are partially constructed texts that allow students to augment with their own original text. These are more sophisticated than the sentence and story starters popularized in teacher workbooks because they furnish a scaffold (literally) in the form of a framework. The writer must consider how his or her words work with the ones already in the model. Unlike a simple story starter, the writer must think both at the micro level (word and sentence) as well as the macro level (the message, voice, and tone of the overall piece).

Using existing writing as a model for new writing is another way to engage young writers. This method was modeled in the popular film *Finding*

Forrester (2000). You may recall from the film that a reclusive author, played by Sean Connery, mentors an accomplished adolescent writer. He requires the young man to copy the opening paragraph of a published essay and then add original writing to the piece. Similarly, writing models provide students with a pattern or scaffold with which to create original writing. Consistent with a gradual-release model (Pearson & Gallagher, 1983) writing from a model requires increased student control over the text and reduced teacher influence.

Four Types of Writing Models

We use these tools to support students as they move toward greater independence in writing: patterned texts, touchstone texts, paragraph frames, and summary writing.

➡ PATTERNED TEXTS

This type of writing model utilizes published texts that possess a unique pattern or characteristic that provides a frame for students to replicate in their own writing. Sequence books that use a repetition to tell a story are especially useful for this kind of model. For example, the book *Fortunately* by Remy Charlip has a wonderful repetition that students find engaging. Based on the familiar playground game, the narrator recounts an adventure through sentences that begin with "Fortunately..." followed by another sentence that starts with "Unfortunately..."

Using this writing model, fifth grader Melia wrote the following:

> Fortunately, I found a sailboat.
> Unfortunately, it had a hole in it.
> Fortunately, I had a bucket.
> Unfortunately, it had a hole in it, too.

Texts that have a sequence of events that are easily transported to other situations invite students to think and write creatively. The plight of the protagonist in the poem *There Was an Old Woman Who Swallowed a Fly* is familiar to most schoolchildren. Melia wrote an adaptation of this poem using a writing model her teacher had constructed.

> There was a young women who borrowed a book.
> I don't know why she borrowed a book.
> She borrowed the book to look up a word.
> She looked up the word to name her new bird.
> She got a new bird to sing a song.
> She sang a song to start her day.
> But I don't know why she started that way.
> Perhaps she'll play.

→ TOUCHSTONE TEXTS

Touchstone texts are an extension of patterned writing models. Like patterned texts, these pieces offer outstanding examples of a device or a technique used by an accomplished author. These may be excerpts from a longer book or the entire book itself. For example, short mysteries like the *Encyclopedia Brown* series by Donald Sobol are great for modeling the use of foreshadowing in the form of clues; Eve Bunting's *Smoky Night* serves as a model for the use of descriptive language; and Ruth Heller's series on the parts of speech introduce parts of speech and their functions in the context of lyrical, engaging sentences. Some texts are better to use to teach sentence writing, others are better to teach text structures and features, while still others are better for teaching specific genres or literary devices. (See page 110 for a list of books we recommend for specific instructional features.)

When using touchstone texts for their patterns or features, be sure to consider your students' interests. Even a wonderfully crafted text is likely to fall short if the subject matter doesn't captivate students and motivate them to try on these techniques for themselves.

TIP

Touchstone Texts

One of our favorite ways to introduce touchstone texts for writing models is by reading the book *Love That Dog* by Sharon Creech. This brief book is the writing journal of a boy named Jack. His teacher loves poetry. Initially, Jack does not love poetry but comes to appreciate it as he uses works by William Carlos Williams, Robert Frost, and Walter Dean Myers as writing models for his own original poems. We read and discuss the elements of the poems and, along with Jack, write our own poems from the models Creech includes.

RECOMMENDED BOOKS FOR WRITING MODELS

FEATURE	TEXT
Story sequence	*Joseph Had a Little Overcoat* by Simms Taback *Somewhere Today: A Book of Peace* by Shelley Moore Thomas *Imagine a Day* by Sarah L. Thomson *The Napping House* by Audrey Wood
Diary	*Diary of a Spider* by Doreen Cronin *Diary of Worm* by Doreen Cronin *Dear America* series
Cause and effect	*If You Give a Mouse a Cookie* by Laura Joffe Numeroff *Fortunately* by Remy Charlip *The Scrambled States of America* by Laurie Keller
Poetry in two voices	*Joyful Noise* by Paul Fleischman *I Am Phoenix* by Paul Fleischman *Math Talk: Mathematical Ideas in Poems for Two Voices* by Theoni Pappas
Using poetry in story form	*Love that Dog* by Sharon Creech *Out of the Dust* by Karen Hesse
Plot (wordless books)	*Tuesday* by David Wiesner *Time Flies* by Eric Rohmann *Window* by Jeannie Baker *The Snowman* by Raymond Briggs
Using quotes to advance plot	*Martin's Big Words* by Doreen Rappaport *John's Secret Dreams: The Life of John Lennon* by Doreen Rappaport *Through My Eyes* by Ruby Bridges
Dialogue	*Ring! Yo?* by Chris Raschka *Don't Let the Pigeon Drive the Bus!* by Mo Willems *Chrysanthemum* by Kevin Henkes
Description	*Because of Winn-Dixie* by Kate DiCamillo *Hope Was Here* by Joan Bauer *Smoky Night* by Eve Bunting
Letter writing as a story device	*P.S. Longer Letter Later* by Paula Danzinger and Ann M. Martin *Dear Mr. Henshaw* by Beverly Cleary *Dear Mr. Blueberry* by Simon James
Dialect	*Saving Sweetness* by Diane Stanley *Cajun Through and Through* by Tynia Thomassie
Surprise endings	*First Day Jitters* by Julie Danneberg *Paper Bag Princess* by Robert Munsch
Opening paragraphs that grab attention	*Holes* by Louis Sachar *Charlotte's Web* by E. B. White *Maniac Magee* by Jerry Spinelli
Writing for information	*Bodyscope: Movers and Shapers* by Patricia McNair *Spiders and Their Webs* by Darlene A. Murawski
How-to writing	*How a Book Is Made* by Aliki *The Klutz Book of Magic* by John Cassidy
Persuasive writing	*Caps for Sale* by Esphyr Slobodkina *The True Story of the Three Little Pigs* by Jon Scieszka *Click, Clack, Moo: Cows That Type* by Doreen Cronin

→ PARAGRAPH FRAMES

A third type of writing model is the paragraph frame. This consists of a series of transitional phrases that serve as a skeletal frame for a paragraph. Since novice writers rarely use transitional phrases to create relationships between the ideas in their paragraph, these frames make it easy for the writer to incorporate them into original text. In addition, the writer must think about the meaning of the transitional words and phrases and relate this to the overall piece. For example, Deasia's teacher gave her the following paragraph frame:

Memorial Day is. . . Memorial Day gave me. . . I also remembered. . . I miss. . . I wonder. . .

Deasia wrote the following:

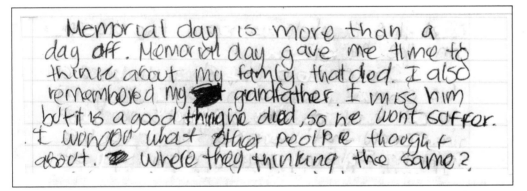

Text: *Memorial Day is more than a day off. Memorial Day gave me time to think about my family that died. I also remembered my grandfather. I miss him but it is a good thing he died, so he won't suffer. I wonder what other people thought about. Were they thinking the same?*

ASSESSMENT LINK

Collect timed writing samples from your students and count the number of transitional words and phrases they use. After teaching paragraph frames, collect another timed sample and compare the differences. If paragraph frames are effective, students should show a steady increase in their writing fluency.

→ SUMMARY WRITING

We use another type of writing model to teach students about writing summaries. The summary is a specific genre of writing, and one that students are asked to do countless times in their academic careers. Generating Interaction between Schema and Text (GIST) is a systematic approach to developing summaries of informational texts. Developed by James Cunningham, GIST is a way for students to write summaries of longer texts. The reading is introduced and discussed and then sectioned into smaller chunks, usually totaling four to six in number. These segments range from a few sentences to a paragraph or two in length, depending on the overall length of the reading. During a second reading, students compose a single sentence that summarizes each segment. Not surprisingly, this summary sentence prompts much discussion as the group crafts and refines it for the most impact. In this way, GIST summary writing parallels the interactive writing process described in Chapter 3. The end result is a summary (or précis) of four to six sentences. This exercise ensures that the summary is shorter than the original piece (an error we see often with inexperienced writers), yet it addresses information from throughout the reading.

Features of Writing Models Lessons

Implementation: Regardless of their genre, writing models provide space for the novice writer to insert his or her voice. Gail Tompkins has outlined some general guidelines that provide an overview of the ways in which different writing models can be used.

- *Explain the model.* After reading the selected text, discuss the model with students by highlighting the features that the author used. This step should clearly establish the purpose of using the selected writing as a model.
- *Share examples.* Provide students with a number of examples of the use of the model. Remember that if you show students only one example, they will likely reproduce it as faithfully as they can and you'll likely end up with thirty slight variations of your example. When you share each example, provide copies for everyone or show the example on an overhead, so everyone can see it.
- *Review the model.* At this point in the lesson, review the key features of the model that students will be using in their writing. This helps them

refocus on the writing model itself and not on replicating the examples you used. (Depending on the text and the number of times students have used writing models, these first three steps may be brief or require an extended amount of time.)

- *Compose collaboratively.* When presenting a new writing model to a group, the teacher scribes an example before students begin to write a group piece together. He or she solicits words and phrases from the group to insert into the writing model. Students watch the text become complete and note the variation of ideas that are permissible in the newly created text. This is consistent with the gradual release of responsibility in that the teacher has modeled a strategy (in this case, the use of a writing model), discussed it, and assisted students in completing the task. At this point, students are ready to complete their group composition.

- *Compose individually.* In this final step, students use what they have been taught via the writing model to develop their own independent writing.

 ## FOLLOW-UP ACTIVITIES

The text that students produce from a writing model can also be extended in ways similar to LEA and interactive writing. For example, teachers may ask students to do the following:

- *illustrate their compositions*

- *add additional independent writing in the form of an extension at the end of the completed writing model*

- *trade papers with a peer and discuss the differences between the two pieces*

- *type final versions for publication*

You may have noticed that this is the first time we've mentioned typed or otherwise published writing. These may be single pieces for display or bound in a collection or anthology created by the class. We're not implying that no student writing is worthy of publication until it reaches this point. There may be times when student-dictated language experience stories or group-composed interactive writing may also be published as a final piece or class book. We're suggesting publication as a follow-up routine with the model-writing approach because students are producing longer pieces of text.

Using Writing Models With the Whole Class

A common example of a writing model is the popular "I am" poem in which students use sentence starters that all focus on one main idea. (Fisher & Drake, 1999; Moretti, 1996). (See page 116 for a reproducible "I am" poem template used in the following example.)

Mr. Schmidt's sixth-grade class works with the "I am" poem model to understand a novel that deals with challenging social studies content: Sonia Levitin's *Dream Freedom* prompts a class discussion about modern-day slavery in the Sudan. The class is moved by a chapter recounting the experience of Aziz, the son of a wealthy man, on his first visit to the slave market with his father. Aziz is horrified to witness the treatment of an enslaved man named Kwol Biong. An excerpt of the class discussion follows:

Nery: Aziz can't believe he saw a man being beaten.

Mr. Schmidt: Everyone look for a sentence or two that lets us know as readers how disgusted he is. The author does a good job of telling us through Aziz's eyes, rather that stating it outright. (The students look back in the text for examples, and Doreathea raises her hand.)

Mr. Schmidt: Let's hear it.

Doreathea: "The slave had not moved or cried out at the beating, but now Aziz saw how his teeth were clenched together. His entire face was a grimace of pain."

Mr. Schmidt: Why did that move you?

Doreathea: I guess 'cause he saw the man as a person, not a thing.

Carlo:: Yeah, that's when he [Aziz] understands that it's not just business.

Mr. Schmidt: You're on to something here. Aziz begins to see these enslaved people as human beings, not property. That's such an important realization for him. He'll never be the same because of this.

Belinda: He's a person like Aziz.

Mr. Schmidt: Right. Exactly. Kwol Biong has a voice. Let's give him one. We can use the "I am" writing frame to create poems about what Kwol might be thinking and feeling.

The students in Mr. Schmidt's class have written "I am" poems before about people in history and characters in stories, and by the next day they have all written one for Kwol Biong. Erik, an English language learner from Argentina, included these sentences in his poem:

- *I am a slave*

- *I wonder who will help me be free*

- *I hear bones brake*

- *I want to see my frend*

Here's an example of the "I am" model used in an eighth-grade classroom. Ms. Kim Lee has selected *Parrot in the Oven: Mi Vida* by Victor Martinez to read with the class. The story revolves around a Latino family in California who struggle with daily hardships and a series of family crises, including substance abuse and domestic violence. At the heart of the story is a 14-year-old boy named Manny, who struggles to keep his family together through it all. Halfway through the novel, Ms. Lee asks her students to write an analysis of the major characters. As part of this essay assignment, she invites students to write an "I am" poem for a character of their choice. Her explanation and a brief class discussion follow:

Ms. Lee: The "I am" poem is a way to capture the voice of a character. I'm giving you a copy of this writing frame so you'll see what I mean. Take a look at it and tell me what you notice about it.

Stephanie: All the lines start with *I*. (The class giggles.)

Ms. Lee: She's right, you know. Let's think deeper. Why is that one word important?

Marcus: It's first person?

Anne: It's the way a person talks about themselves.

Ms. Lee: There you go. Yes. When we talk about writer's craft, we call it voice. The voice of a character is what makes him or her unique. The "I am" poem is in first person, like Marcus said. It's a way to give voice to a character. What else do you notice?

Brian: There's senses, like hear and see.

Elise: And feel. That can be a sense, too. Like if you're touching something.

Ms. Lee: So, in an "I am" poem there's a place for sensory images as well. Anything else? What do some of those other words get you thinking about?

Marcus: Well, thinking. There're words in here that are about thinking.

Ms. Lee: Like what? Tell me more.

Shanequa: There's words that can only be answered if you know what the person's thinking. Like *understand* and *wonder*. If you can't answer that, you don't really have a good idea about the person.

STANZAS FOR AN "I AM" POEM

1. I am (special characteristics or nouns about you)

2. I wonder (something you are curious about)

3. I hear (an imaginary sound)

4. I want (an actual desire of yours)

5. I am (repeat first line of poem)

6. I pretend (something you pretend to do)

7. I feel (an imaginary feeling)

8. I touch (an imaginary touch)

9. I worry (something that truly bothers you)

10. I cry (something that makes you very sad)

11. I am (repeat the first line of the poem)

12. I understand (something you know is true)

13. I say (something that you believe in)

14. I dream (something you dream about)

15. I try (something you make an effort about)

16. I hope (something you actually hope for)

17. I am (repeat the first line of the poem)

From "Writing Instruction for Struggling Adolescent Readers: A Gradual Release Model." D. Fisher and N. Frey. Copyright © 2003 by D. Fisher and N. Frey. Reprinted by permission of the *Journal of Adolescent and Adult Literacy*.

Ms. Lee: Thanks—I agree. So, let's review. With an "I am" poem, you're giving a character a voice by using first person. You've got to come up with some sensory images. Very important in writing, using imagery. And you've got to get inside the head of the character to think like he or she thinks. How are you going to accomplish that?

Stephanie: You can look in the book? Like for quotes?

Ms. Lee: Sure you can. That's one way. But keep in mind that not all the characters are going to talk right at you this way. How else can you give a character voice?

DeJuan: You have to know what they did. And why they did it. You know— their behavior.

Ms. Lee: Bingo! That's it! Pay attention to your character's behavior. It will help you to understand their voice.

Shanequa writes the following "I am" poem from the point of view of Magda, Manny's 16-year-old sister, who discovers she is pregnant and later loses the baby.

I am Magda.

I wonder what my baby would of looked like.

I hear my mom and dad arguing.

I see my baby dying.

I want to close my eyes and never wake up.

I am Magda.

I pretend that someday we will have money.

I feel bored because I have to work.

I touch my stomach, thinking about my baby.

I worry that we will get poor and won't have food.

I cry every night.

I am Magda.

I understand what I'm going thru.

I say what's on my mind.

I dream someday we could be rich.

I try to help my family.

I hope everything will be okay.

I am Magda.

Fourth-grade teacher Ms. Hernandez uses a patterned text to inspire her students' writing. Her students, many of whom are of Middle Eastern and Eastern European descent, possess a sophisticated level of knowledge about the conflict in the Middle East. It's a topic of conversation at dinner tables and in the small stores that dot the busy avenues of the neighborhood. Therefore, Ms. Hernandez has incorporated this topic into her classroom curriculum. At the beginning of the year, they developed class norms for interacting with one another respectfully, especially when disagreeing. The class has adopted a motto: *We are all peacemakers in our world.*

They've read a variety of books about peace this year. One, *Somewhere Today: A Book of Peace* by Shelley Moore Thomas, is a patterned text. Each page of the book contains a sentence that starts with "Somewhere today" and pictures a common experience from the world over such as fixing toys and planting trees. Following a discussion of several recent articles from the weekly classroom magazine that Ms. Hernandez subscribes to, she read aloud the book to the class.

Then she asks each student to use the sentence starter "Somewhere today . . ." and write one to three sentences about peace in the Middle East. Each student types his or her sentences on the classroom computer, illustrates them with original drawings, clipart, or magazine pictures. The final products are bound into a class book. Here are some examples from the book:

- *Somewhere today a baby was saved in the hospital.*
- *Somewhere today a Palestinian put down a bomb and called a friend.*
- *Somewhere today they are having meetings to talk peace.*
- *Somewhere today a girl gets flowers and is happy.*

Ms. Hernandez often creates class books using writing models. She says, "What I like about this strategy is that they see the product of their discussions and work. We do lots of independent writing, but I also want them to see that some of our best work is created together."

TIP

Group Editing

To model the editing decisions needed to assemble a class compilation book, display all the pages at once on the whiteboard, using magnets to make reorganization easy. Read aloud the entire book first, then invite students to comment on particularly strong opening and concluding pages. They'll find it easier to identify the beginning and ending first because these tend to be the most dominant. Work through the book, filling in the order. Rearrange each page and reread from the beginning so students hear the pacing and cadence of the book. Young writers are often reluctant to edit their own work for fear they will have to "do it over." These group editing experiences help them appreciate the benefits of this necessary process.

Using Writing Models With Small Groups

Ms. Takahashi meets with a small group of third-grade students at her teacher center to work with a writing model. Through her analysis of writing samples, she's observed that the students in this group struggle with word choice. Using her classroom rubric, she's noted that they struggle with three elements of word choice:

- First, they don't vary their words. Instead, they rely on stock vocabulary such as *nice, like*, and *said* to describe.

- Second, they're less likely than their fluent peers to use technical vocabulary in their writing, even when they've had targeted vocabulary instruction.

- Third, their word choices are sometimes incorrect or inappropriate.

As one of her interventions, Ms. Takahashi decides that the members of this group will produce acrostic poems, which will aid them in word selection. In an effort to increase their vocabulary capacity, she uses thematic alphabet books to get them writing. They've been studying about plants in science, so Ms. Takahashi has decided that they will develop an ABC acrostic poem about that topic. She begins by introducing the assignment to Austin, Charlotte, Victor, and Fatima and then distributes an A–Z chart like the one shown on page 121.

Ms. Takahashi: Let's begin by brainstorming words that have to do with plants. Think about words you've learned in science. One word I can think of is *stem*. I can write that word in the box for the letter *S*. Who has another?

Fatima: *Plant.*

Ms. Takahashi: Okay, put that in the box for *P*. Let's see if we can find a word for each box.

After several more examples are generated by the group, the students settle into the task. In a few minutes, they have all recorded some words. However, many boxes remain blank. Ms. Takahashi assures them that they will have some new words to add after she reads *A Gardener's Alphabet* by Mary Azarian with them. The words used in this alphabet book are not easy. It includes terms like *arbor, manure,* and *topiary*. Using this book as a model, each of the young writers adds more words to their list. They round out their list with additional words from their science textbook. Later, for homework, they'll add additional words to the boxes.

The next day, the group returns to Ms. Takahashi with a bank of words for their acrostic poem. She shows them how to turn their word list into a poem about plants.

Ms. Takahashi: You've all got at least three words in each box, except maybe for harder letters like *Q* and *X*. Writers know lots of words and use them in their writing to make it interesting for the reader. Now you're going to use these words to make a poem. You'll use a word from each box to begin a phrase or sentence with each letter of the alphabet. Victor, give me an *A* word for us to get started.

Victor: *A* like in *apple*, because it's a plant, a tree.

Ms. Takahashi: You can use that, Victor. The first line of your poem could be *Apples grow on trees*. Who's got a word beginning with *B*?

Austin: I do! *B* is for *bud*.

Ms. Takahashi: And what does a bud do?

Austin: It's the beginning of a flower.

Charlotte: Or a leaf. A bud can turn into a leaf.

Ms. Takahashi: Oh, I like that! It could be the second line: *Buds are the beginning of leaves and flowers.*

After getting the group started on an acrostic poem, Ms. Takahashi sends the students back to their seats for independent writing. She reminds them to use words from their lists to make the poems interesting.

Over time, the students in this group select an array of themes: Ian selects the topic of music and includes the words *CD player*, *note*, *orchestra*, and *piano;* Charlotte chooses animals as her theme and includes the words *bear*, *giraffe*, and *skunk;* and Fatima decides on cooking and includes *bake*, *mix*, *oven*, *spices*, and *vegetables* in her A–Z chart. This variety of themes allows them to add words, and pages, to their writing vocabulary resource list (see Assessment Link, page 122).

Fifth-grade teacher Mr. Hardiman uses a paragraph frame (e.g., Oja, 1996) as a writing model in his social studies curriculum. His class is focused on "Wagons West"—a unit of study about the westward movement. He meets with small groups of students, at least one group per day, to extend content instruction. This way, Mr. Hardiman sees each student in his or her small group at least weekly. He's told us that "it's a good way to make sure I'm having academic conversations with all of my students."

Everything I know about _____

A	B	C	D	E
F	G	H	I	J
K	L	M	N	O
P	Q	R	S	T
U	V	W	X	Y
Z				

ASSESSMENT LINK

As you've seen from Ms. Takahashi's work, vocabulary resource lists such as the A–Z Chart on page 121 are useful for younger writers or those who find more formal resources like a thesaurus too cumbersome. They are also an excellent source of assessment data, because you can gauge their vocabulary knowledge and make instructional decisions. Begin by reproducing a blank A-Z chart for each writer and then introduce a topic for the day's writing that is related to a current unit of study (for example, the Gold Rush). Give students five to ten minutes to write all the terms they associate with the Gold Rush, such as *Sutter's Mill* and *rich*. Make sure that students understand that they should record words as they think of them, and not in alphabetical order, which will slow them down. When they are finished, take a look at the terms they have recorded and note when critical terms such as *Forty-Niners* or *Eureka!* are missing. These results provide valuable insight into what each child knows and does not know and will allow you to use your instructional time for what is needed, without wasting time on concepts students already know. After teaching the missing content, return the A–Z charts to the students and ask them to add any new terms. A further assessment benefit for you is that you can gain valuable information about the effectiveness of your teaching. In addition, your students will have developed a word bank to refer to for future writing about the topic.

Mr. Hardiman begins with conversation and a review of life on the Oregon Trail. He reads aloud a passage from Paul Erikson's book *Daily Life in a Covered Wagon* and points out how the author has used descriptive language about when the Larkin family crossed a river. Mr. Hardiman tells them that they're going to write a paragraph for the Larkin family diary: "I'm going to give you some connecting words—transition words—to tie your paragraph together."

On a small dry erase board, he outlines the following story:

There I was on the trail. I couldn't believe … I was …
Just as I was about to give up hope … Thankfully, …
+ 2 sentences

(The students in this group know that an ellipsis […] means that they are to add their own text to complete the sentence.)

Sinh, a student in the group, writes the following:

> There I was on the trail. I couldn't believe how hot it was. Why did I leave in July? I was sweating and I had no more water. Just as I was about to give up hope I came to a pond. Thankfully, the water was clean and I ~~came to a pond.~~ could drink it. Then we were ready to go to California,

Text: *There I was on the trail. I couldn't believe how hot it was. Why did I leave in July? I was sweating and I had no more water. Just as I was about to give up hope I came to a pond. Thankfully, the water was clean and I could drink it. Then, we were ready to go to California.*

Mr. Hardiman has remarked to us that his students often add more than what's required to these paragraphs. "I find that if they've got some good background knowledge, and I make the paragraph frame interesting, they'll take off. What I like about paragraph frames is that they seem to be just the boost that lots of these really good writers need."

Using Writing Models With Individual Students

Using writing models is an excellent way to individualize instruction for students. Working individually with a student provides the teacher an opportunity to understand the student's composing and encoding processes. A simple writing model is the story pyramid. This writing model is used to provide a concrete structure and is well suited for students who prefer specific instructions about writing. This is an ideal model for working individually with students who need instruction on story structure or grammar.

Ms. James uses a story pyramid following the format on page 124 with Daniel, a student with a disability in her third-grade class. Daniel doesn't particularly enjoy writing, and he finds the fluid parameters of writing assignments difficult. Ms. James wants Daniel to write more in response to their readings and has chosen a story pyramid as a means to help him get a summary on paper. Using this type of writing model provides Ms. James

_____
(name of the main character)

_____
(2 words describing the main character)

_____
(3 words describing the setting)

_____
(4 words stating the problem)

_____
(5 words describing one event)

_____
(6 words describing another event)

_____
(7 words describing another event)

_____
(8 words describing the solution)

the opportunity to teach Daniel about characters, setting, problems, and solution.

During one meeting, she reads *A Bad Case of Stripes* by David Shannon to Daniel. The story recounts the misadventures of Camilla, a young girl who loves lima beans but cares more about being popular. Since all her classmates dislike lima beans, she vows to stop eating them completely. Camilla comes down with a strange malady that causes her skin and clothes to change colors and reflect patterns from her environment. Of course, the cure comes when she resumes eating lima beans, learning a valuable lesson about the importance of staying true to oneself. Ms. James chose this book because she knew it would appeal to Daniel's sense of humor. In addition, the linear nature of the storyline promised to be an easy one for Daniel to follow and summarize.

Based on the reading and their discussion, Daniel writes the following using the story pyramid:

Camilla

pretty, scared

school, home, bedroom

She hates lima beans?

Camilla gets sick. No school!

The doctor says go to school.

Kids tease Camilla and she turns colors.

Camilla eats lima beans and is better again.

Daniel's pyramid story serves as a summary of *A Bad Case of Stripes*. Ms. James can use this as an assessment of his comprehension as well as his understanding of basic elements of story grammar. Ms. James also sometimes uses story pyramids with Daniel as a way to outline more detailed compositions. Each line serves as the basis for a sentence or idea, and the structure keeps Daniel organized in his writing.

Writing models like patterned and touchstone texts, paragraph frames, and summary writing frames such as GIST and pyramid stories provide young writers with structures that move them toward independent writing. Unlike formulaic writing, which is often used as an isolated writing activity, writing models are used as part of a developmental writing program that relies on a gradual release of responsibility. Thus, writing models are not always viewed as a final product but rather as a stepping stone to more sophisticated writing.

❖ ❖ ❖

Background on Research

There is fairly extensive research on the use of writing models. These models include text frames, poems, and other graphic organizers that visually prompt student composition (e.g., McElveen & Dierking, 2000/2001; Staal, 2001). Calfee, Chambliss, and Beretz (1991) noted that writing models help struggling writers improve not only their writing skills but also their confidence in writing. This point should not be overlooked in considering the use of writing models. Too often, intermediate and middle school students have internalized weak and restrictive models of their own that result in unimaginative writing. Writing models serve as a bridge to more original writing; they offer skeletal frameworks from which students can build paragraphs, poems, and summaries. At the same time, don't limit your teaching with writing models to your work with struggling writers. There is evidence that using writing models is an effective way to teach poetry writing (Koch, 1997), story writing (Greene, 1994; Sipe, 1993), and reports (Charney & Carlson, 1995) for all writers.

KEY POINTS
ABOUT WRITING MODELS LESSONS

First and foremost, the writing selected as a model must be interesting and relevant to the students. Revising and reproducing boring or irrelevant text will not engage students in learning to write well. Second, students must understand the task and may need to be told that they are supposed to copy the words from the model and make those words their own. Teacher modeling remains essential throughout a developmental approach to writing, and students need instruction and modeling before being asked to produce any new form of writing. In addition, writing models lessons should do the following:

• *be based on the identified needs of students*

• *encourage individual voice and choice in writing*

• *build self-esteem as students see themselves as writers*

Independent Writing and Authentic Writing Tasks

OBJECTIVE: To create original texts that are purposeful, accurate, and well-crafted

ACTIVITY: Students independently compose a piece of writing using a synthesis of skills they've learned about the conventions and craft of writing.

LEVEL OF SUPPORT: Minimal

INSTRUCTIONAL FORMAT: Individual students

We've finally arrived at the place where you want your students to be—writing independently and well for a variety of purposes. Creativity and originality take their places alongside the conventions of writing as well. And yet ... does independent writing simply occur? Is it just a matter of providing opportunities to write?

Of course not. Our colleagues Leif Fearn and Nancy Farnan often say that there's more to writing than simply causing it, and we agree. We've shown how to integrate six important developmental approaches to writing into your teaching to help students build the skills and strategies young writers need to write independently, especially at the sentence and paragraph levels. All of these approaches demand varying degrees of teacher support.

However, independent writing ultimately needs to be just that—independent. Unlike the other teaching approaches profiled in the book thus far, independent writing doesn't rely on teacher modeling in the same ways. Therefore, the structure of this chapter will be a departure from the others as we address the necessary supports for independent writing. The hard work still falls upon the writer; nonetheless, carefully crafted supports can make that work easier.

In the following section, we'll discuss the "three C's" of support we believe are necessary to sustain young writers in the classroom. These supports are:

- **Curricular:** effective writing prompts and RAFT writing for perspective
- **Collaborative:** peer responses
- **Coaching:** conferring with the teacher

Then, at the end of this chapter, we'll describe a unit of instruction leading to an independent writing assignment that we've used in our classroom. As you'll see, this unit includes aspects of the gradual-release model of writing instruction profiled in this book.

Sustaining Writers Through Curricular Support

We'd like to think that all we have to do is offer very general directions for an independent writing assignment and then send students off to toil away until they emerge with something astounding. After all, how often have we heard the admonition to "write what you know"? (We may even have told our students this.) While it's true that you should "write what you know," most young writers are going to need more structure than that in independent writing.

→ WRITING PROMPTS

One of the most common ways this is accomplished is through the use of writing prompts. We're not talking about the overused and often banal directions given on standardized writing texts. (Our nomination would be a state writing prompt a few years ago that asked fourth graders to imagine they had found an elephant and then describe a day with their new pet!) Instead, we encourage the design of writing prompts and assignments that meet the following criteria:

- *a topic that encourages many kinds of responses, not just one fixed reply*

- *a prompt that allows for a range of writing abilities*
- *instruction that considers the writers' experiences, both in life and the curriculum*
- *a topic that interests the writers*

The first criteria simply means to avoid constrained prompts that result in only one "right" answer, often one perceived as being the teacher-pleasing answer. For example, asking eighth graders to write about "what they'd like to learn in this class" is likely to result in less-than-sincere responses. The other three criteria focus on the learners themselves. Knowing our students, their background knowledge, and their abilities will lead us to develop the best writing assignments for them. In some cases, we use prompts only once, because they fit a particular group of students particularly well at a particular time. Pulitzer Prize–winning author Frank McCourt, who taught writing to adolescents for 30 years in the New York City public schools, tells a story about being inspired by a drawer full of students' forged excuse notes from home:

> Isn't it remarkable, I thought, how they resist any kind of writing assignment in class or at home. They whine and say they're busy and it's hard putting two hundred words together on any subject. But when they forge these excuse notes they're brilliant. Why? I have a drawer full of excuse notes that could be turned into an anthology of Great American Excuses or Great American Lies. (*Teacher Man: A Memoir*, 2005)

In a moment that McCourt describes as "an epiphany," he creates a series of writing prompts asking students to write excuse notes for people in history and literature. Adam and Eve, Al Capone, and Attila the Hun all are given the opportunity to offer excuses for their deeds. He reports that these assignments invigorated his classroom that year as lively debate, impassioned writing, and full participation reigned.

We're not saying that McCourt found the Perfect Writing Prompt. To the contrary, this wouldn't work in many classrooms. But McCourt did understand something about his students and what might interest this particular group. He provided the opportunity to write in a way that resonated with them and then got out of the way.

Another version of writing prompts can come from the use of visuals. We often tell students to use imagery in their writing—visuals can help them accomplish just that by stimulating the use of visual memory. We've used posters, photographs, works of art, excerpts from comic strips and graphic novels—anything to inspire young writers. The use of single images, or even a series of panels from a comic strip, can encourage them to explore worlds outside of their own personal experiences. For example, in a seventh-grade classroom, Mr. Hernandez shows a 1940s black-and-white photograph of a Latino man in a suit and hat who was carrying a black leather medical bag. He asks his students to imagine a scene in which this man might appear. Where was he headed? What would he do once he arrived? Miguel writes the following story response:

> When Dr. Camarillo arrived, Carmen's mother and sisters were taking care of the little girl. Dr. Camarillo, with no words, headed towards the young girl. The parents were comforting each other. The doctor put ice on Carmen's left eye after stitching her forehead. According to Carmen's parents, she fell off the horse and hit a small boulder. Dr. Camarillo desperately waited for Carmen's reaction.

Miguel has the beginnings of a good story here. He's created a scene and a circumstance. His use of the word *desperately* suggests that there might be something else going on, although it's not yet clear to the reader; however, these are points that can be refined later in peer editing and teacher conferring. What's of interest in this example is the use of a single photograph to inspire.

→ RAFT WRITING

The secret to a good writing prompt or assignment is to imbue it with purpose and authenticity. We've mentioned in Chapter 6 that we avoid the use of five-paragraph essays, hamburger paragraphs, and other types of writing that rely too much on a formula. Having said that, we do recognize the need for some structure as young writers create original pieces. One of our favorite ways to accomplish this is through RAFT writing.

RAFT writing, developed by Carol Santa and Lynn Havens, is a method for teaching perspective and voice in writing. RAFT stands for the following:

Role

Audience

Format

Topic

It describes the considerations a writer undertakes in composing a piece of writing.

The RAFT structure provides the teacher with a means for giving a foundation to original student writing while allowing for creative expression. This is especially important for younger writers who are learning about perspective taking. As W. S. Ong points out, for many of our younger or less experienced writers, perspective is difficult because the audience is imaginary.

RAFT Writing in Action: Ms. Allen's fifth-grade class is immersed in a social studies unit on the Holocaust. Her students have been reading novels and nonfiction in their literature circles, including *The Diary of Anne Frank*, *The Devil's Arithmetic*, and *Number the Stars*. Ms. Allen writes the following RAFT assignment on the board:

R: a Jewish child in peril

A: a potential host family

F: letter

T: please hide me from the Nazis

In this RAFT assignment, the writer must determine his or her role in the piece (a Jewish child in need), and the audience being addressed (a family). He or she must also make a decision about the format of the writing (a letter) and the topic (the need for a place to hide).

Ms. Allen instructs her students: "By now, you know about many people and events important to World War II. Today, you get to put yourselves in Europe during that time. I want you to think about the children you've encountered in your literature circles. Look at the board and think about what your role is, who your audience is, what format you should use, and what your topic is."

Students work on this RAFT for about thirty minutes, consult-

TIP

Using Picture Books With RAFT

Ms. Allen has used RAFT writing many times before—that's why she's now able to use it as an independent writing prompt. She first introduced RAFT writing by modeling its use with picture books. The picture book stories gave her students a context for creating a piece with a point of view. For example, earlier in the year they read the wordless picture book *Tuesday* by David Wiesner. The story of flying frogs that make mischief in an unsuspecting town unfolds through captivating illustrations. Ms. Allen modeled writing using the following RAFT:

R TV reporter

A TV viewers

F news report

T what happened last night!

We've included a list of RAFT writing frames you can use with picture books on page 133. Once students are comfortable with the format, you can write these RAFTs on stickie notes and attach them to the inside cover of each book. We keep a shelf of these in our classrooms, as we require a completed RAFT each week from our students.

Feb. 15, 1941

Dear Jasons, My family
Please hide the. Being what
I am can kill me and
my family. We are also
humans, we have two eyes,
arms, legs and fingers. We
should be able to live
and be what we
want to be. Our family
should be like any
others. We all look alike
we haven't done anything
wrong! So please support
us.

Love,
Maggie

Dear sir or Maddam,   5/11/1940

        I am a Jewish child who
needs a place to hide. I want a good
future, but I can't have one, because
they are gathering jewish people
to camps. I want to hide but
I don't have a family. My parents
were taken along with my brothers.
So can you provide me a home
and a place to hide please? Right
now I'm in danger, please help me.

                    Sincerly yours,

                    Joe

ing their social studies textbooks and their literature circle books for details. (RAFT writing offers an opportunity for students to consolidate both content knowledge and composition skills to create a cohesive piece.)

When students use RAFT writing, the teacher's role is minimized. The teacher develops the frame to foster perspective taking in writing, but it's the students who must assume an identity, voice, and point of view. In addition, they also must consider the conventions related to the format and to the composition of the message. Notice that Maggie and Joe each approach the assignment from different angles. Maggie reminds her audience that people are more alike than different from one another. Joe makes sure his audience understands his plight and appeals to their sense of compassion for a child. In both cases, Joe and Maggie incorporate content knowledge and their unique voices to create original and compelling pieces of independent writing.

Maggie and Joe use different reasoning to appeal to the families.

SAMPLE PICTURE BOOK RAFTS

CASEY AT THE BAT (Thayer and Bing, 2001)	THE BIG BOX (Morrison, 1999)	ROUGH-FACE GIRL (Martin, 1992)
R Sports reporter A Mudville fans F Newspaper article T Mudville loses	R Patty, Mickey, or LizaSue A Adults F A speech T What my freedom means to me	R Cinderella A Rough-Face Girl F Letter T Our sisters
YEH SHEN: A CINDERELLA STORY FROM CHINA (Louie, 1999)	VOICES IN THE PARK (Browne, 2001)	A PICTURE BOOK OF LOUIS BRAILLE (Adler, 1997)
R Cinderella A Yeh-Shen F Letter T Our sisters	R 1st voice A 2nd voice F Letter T You don't belong in my park	R Louis Braille A National Institute F Business letter T Please adopt my new system of writing
TUESDAY (Weisner, 1991)	MRS. KATZ & TUSH (Polacco, 1994)	THE KOREAN CINDERELLA (Climo, 1993)
R Police officer A Department captain F Incident report T Tuesday night's incidents	R Larnel A Mourners F Eulogy T Goodbye, Mrs. Katz	R Pear Blossom A Stepmother F Goodbye note T I'm leaving
TUESDAY (Weisner, 1991)	BEETLE BOY (David, 1999)	I'M IN CHARGE OF CELEBRATIONS (Baylor, 1995)
R TV reporter A Viewers F News report T What happened last night	R Gregory A Mom and Dad F Note T Why don't you notice me?	R Desert girl A Me, myself, and I F Book entry T Today's celebration
TAR BEACH (Ringgold, 1991)	THE LIBRARY (Stewart, 1995)	RICHARD WRIGHT & THE LIBRARY CARD (Miller, 1999)
R Cassie A Diary F Diary entry T The view from up here	R Elizabeth Brown A The town F Donation form T I'm giving you my books	R Sponsor A Librarian F Letter T Give Richard a library card
SMOKY NIGHT (Bunting, 1999)	TOMÁS AND THE LIBRARY LADY (Mora, 1997)	RICHARD WRIGHT & THE LIBRARY CARD (Miller, 1999)
R Daniel A Mrs. Kim F Invitation T Our neighborhood after the riot	R Tomás A The library lady F Letter T Thank you	R Protestor A Librarian F Letter T No card for African-Americans!

Sustaining Writers Through Collaborative Support From Peers

Most professional writers include an acknowledgement of thanks to their editor (thank you, Sarah Glasscock and Sarah Longhi!) and with good reason—editors are great at asking questions that cause writers to think about their writing in a different way. These questions and comments can lead to better prose, especially at the hands of a skilled editor. After all, consider the word *revision—re-vision*. An editor can help us re-envision our writing. Our classrooms are no different. For every writer in your class, there are twenty, thirty, or more editors ready to help a fellow writer think differently about his or her writing—they just may not know it. Our job is to teach students how to be good editors for one another.

Many of us have attempted peer editing in our classrooms before, only to think "I'll never try that again!" Countless times we've seen students providing vague and decidedly unhelpful feedback like this:

- "This is good." (confusing good manners with editing)

- "This stinks." (confusing criticism with editing)

- "You're not a good writer." (confusing disparagement with editing)

Thankfully, we don't see much of the last type, but we certainly see quite a bit of the first two. In the absence of knowing how to offer editing advice, most students vacillate between the If You Don't Have Anything Nice to Say, Don't Say Anything at All school of editing, and its sister institution, If I'm Criticizing, I'm Doing My Job belief system. It takes teaching and practice to avoid these approaches.

We really think of peer editing as peer response. Students need to know and understand what peer response sounds like. This means that it should first be modeled and practiced by the teacher so that students begin to grasp the purpose.

As we explain in Chapter 2, we've incorporated Jay Simmons' work on peer response in our assessment model. We've used his system for categorizing types of responses that are helpful to fellow writers, such as drawing in the writer through personal questions ("Did that really happen to you?") and offering feedback on the needs of a reader ("This paragraph is confusing. I'm having trouble understanding what you mean"). The Types of Peer

Response chart on page 51 contains a complete chart of peer responses to use with your students as you teach peer response. In addition, the Techniques to Teach Peer Responses chart on page 52 offers Simmons' teaching points for modeling peer responses for editing.

There are several principles to consider when planning for peer response in the classroom. Perhaps the most crucial one is that the sessions should be invited by the writer, not prescribed through a one-size-fits-all classroom schedule. Our experience has been that mandatory peer response is halfhearted at best, with both parties more concerned about checking off a box than offering or receiving any real help.

In addition, the focus of a peer response conference should be on the needs of a reader. Each editor is a reader first, and a reader's impressions, confusions, and delights are rich material for a young writer. The details of the piece such as ideas, conventions, word choice, organization, sentence fluency, voice, and presentation are truly the function of a full-fledged editor (you) and should come during teacher-student writing conferences (more on that in the next section). Encourage students to talk with one another as readers, not critics. When something they read makes them laugh, feel sad, or think, they should tell the writer so, and explain why. This type of feedback is useful and appreciated by young writers, who typically view their peers as a primary audience anyway.

TIP

Fishbowl Technique
Use a fishbowl technique to allow the entire class to listen in on two students and to evaluate the peer response conference.

ASSESSMENT LINK

Peer response conferences provide an excellent opportunity to collect assessment information. Teach peer editors to record ideas and questions they have about a piece of writing in preparation for a conference with the writer. You may want to offer them a structured response form like the one on page 136. Notice that this form includes space for the reader's notes as well as the writer's reactions to those responses, which can spur the writer to make a plan for revision. Completed peer response forms allow you to monitor the content of the peer editing conversations as well as learn how to better support the writer.

PEER RESPONSE CONFERENCE FORM

Reader:_____ Date:_____

MY IDEAS AND QUESTIONS

Title of Piece: _____ Writer: _____

REACTIONS

• *My favorite part...*

_____

_____

_____

• *I understood...*

_____

_____

_____

• *I wonder...*

_____

_____

_____

• *Have you thought about...*

_____

_____

_____

• *The next thing you might do is...*

_____

_____

_____

Sustaining Writers Through Coaching

The issues around ideas, conventions, word choice, organization, sentence fluency, voice, and presentation are still important. After all, you've been teaching these throughout this gradual-release approach to writing, even when you haven't explicitly named them as such. These elements, known collectively as 6 + 1 traits of writing, were discussed in detail in Chapter 2 on assessment. Here's a reminder about each trait:

1. *Ideas: the central message or topic*

2. *Organization: the structure of the piece*

3. *Voice: the ways in which the writer communicates thoughts, feelings, and ideas*

4. *Word Choice: the way the vocabulary reflects the writer's message*

5. *Sentence Fluency: the way the sentences and paragraphs "hang together"*

6. *Conventions: spelling, grammar, punctuation, and mechanics*

+1. *Presentation: the appearance, layout, or delivery of the piece*

There is perhaps no finer way to support young writers than to confer with them about their writing. These sessions are an ideal time to coach them individually as they craft their original ideas. Conferring is not just for independent writing, of course. Effective teachers use conferring as the backbone of their literacy instruction. In writing, this most often comes after the writer has met with a peer to gauge a response to his or her writing. After the peer response conference, the writer can edit and revise the piece. The teacher serves as a writing coach, helping the student process feedback, reflect on their writing processes, and make decisions about the next steps.

Diane Barone and Joan Taylor say that "the three hardest challenges in helping student writers . . . are getting them started, keeping them going, and getting them finished" (2006). That's a great summary of the purposes of coaching through conferring. Individual conferences, often no more than a few minutes long, can provide just the boost that young writers need to see their piece through. It's important to note that coaching conferences are not dependent on a particular approach to writing, such as writing workshop. Regardless of your method for organizing your classroom, you want to make sure you're creating time and space for yourself to meet individually with writers. Without this type of support, the gradual release of responsibility model is not fully realized.

TIP

Sign-Up Sheet
Keep your schedule organized by posting a sign-up sheet for coaching conferences. Include the date, name, and topic of the conference. This also serves as a simple form of record-keeping to alert you to writers who may be avoiding these conferences.

Because these coaching conferences last only a few minutes, it's useful to limit the focus of an individual meeting. We use this sequence in our coaching conferences:

- *Inquiry: The opening of the conference includes questions about the student's current writing, especially the topic, the status of the piece, and areas of difficulty.*

- *Decisions: Based on the response from the student, the teacher makes choices about the focus of the conference.*

- *Instruction: The teacher chooses a point for teaching. This may include any of the 6 + 1 traits and incorporates a plan for next steps for the writer.*

- *Next Steps: The teacher logs anecdotal notes on the conference for follow-up.*

The Coaching Conference form on page 140 provides a simple template for recordkeeping.

→ **COACHING CONFERENCE IN ACTION**

A coaching conference between third-grade teacher Ms. Guthrie and 8-year-old Martha focused on the beginning of an autobiographical incident Martha was writing on learning to ride a bike.

Ms. Guthrie: Tell me about your memory piece. How is it going?

Martha: Okay. I have some ideas written down. Sanji [a classmate] helped me.

Ms. Guthrie: Let's see what you've got so far. (She reads Martha's draft.)

Ms. Guthrie: It looks like you've made a list. You're planning your story?

Martha: Yeah, I wrote it in order.

Ms. Guthrie: That's a great start. It seems like your next step will be to turn these points into sentences.

Martha: Uh-huh.

Ms. Guthrie: You can't just string these together, though, can you? It would sound funny. (She begins to read Martha's list aloud.) I got a new bike. The new bike had training wheels.

Martha: (giggles) Yeah, it's choppy!

Ms. Guthrie: It sure is. So, you want to make these sentences flow together. You'll probably be writing new sentences in between to make it flow. Let's look at your first two sentences. You could combine them to make a more interesting sentence. Try it to see what it sounds like.

(Martha tries several combinations, settling on *I got a new bike with training wheels.*)

Ms. Guthrie: What are you going to do next?

Martha: I'm going to write it in paragraphs.

Ms. Guthrie: And remember that you'll need to add sentences in between sometimes.

Martha: So it sounds good.

Ms. Guthrie: Yes, so it sounds good. So, let's talk again when you're ready.

Martha brought these notes to her coaching conference with Ms. Guthrie.

→ A WARNING ABOUT TEACHER FEEDBACK

We'd be remiss if we failed to address the "dark side" of teacher feedback on writing. Researchers have raised ethical questions regarding the fine line between support and intrusion. At what point does a student's writing cease to be his or her own because a teacher has altered it so extensively? Linda Darling Hammond uses the term "ventriloquism" to describe the phenomenon of a voice that has shifted from the writer to the editor. As teachers, we must balance our feedback so that it remains helpful without changing it to the point of being unrecognizable. We want our students to value writing as a form of expression; it is incumbent upon us to offer ethical responses to our students' writing, being sensitive to the tremendous influence we have over them. Sam Patterson, co-director of the San Diego Writing Project, makes these recommendations:

- *Don't write on their drafts.*

- *Respond as a reader; remember they need a reader's perspective more than an editor's.*

- *Ask questions that will encourage deeper thinking, and provide motivation for revision (2005).*

COACHING CONFERENCE RECORDKEEPING FORM

Name _____ Date: _____

Title of Piece: _____

Author: _____

Focus: _____

INQUIRY:

DECISIONS:

INSTRUCTION:

NEXT STEPS:

While independent writing is, by definition, independent, the role of the teacher is no less important. He or she organizes the supports (curricular, collaborative, and coaching assistance) necessary to help students get started, keep going, and finish (to paraphrase Barone and Taylor). Of course, juggling all these phases of writing development can be a bit daunting. In the next section, we'll describe an independent writing project we completed with our students—a group of adolescents who had been identified as "at risk" of not passing their grade-level competencies.

Scaffolding Independent Writing for Struggling Writers: A Photo Essay Book Project*

The construction paper, photographs, glue sticks, and scissors strewn across the desks suggest a scene from a typical middle school classroom. However, there are other clues that disclose the real identities of the students. The bookshelves contain titles like *I Know Why the Caged Bird Sings* by Maya Angelou and *Learning Outside the Lines* by Jonathan M. Mooney and David Cole. This week's word wall features the words *malice, malodorous, malevolent, malaria,* and *malpractice.* Flyers for the after-school tutoring program and a teen hotline are pinned to the bulletin board. While the materials evoke memories of early learning experiences, the work of these students is sophisticated and complex. They are immersed in a creative writing project using photos they've taken with disposable cameras. The task requires them to produce an original work of fiction illustrated with photos.

Every morning, students are greeted with bellwork (Wong & Wong, 2001) as they arrive in class: a writing prompt has been posted on the whiteboard. Everyone is writing in response to the prompt by the time class has begun. This is followed immediately by three one-minute rounds of a fluency-building practice of Power Writing. Thus, students have written an average of 200 words daily within the first ten minutes of class—quite an accomplishment for these once-reluctant writers.

After this morning routine, the class settles into the work of the day. In keeping with the gradual-release model, students progress through targeted lessons using interactive writing for adolescents, generative writing, and writing models. The class also uses the RAFT writing models as frames to

*This activity description was adapted from an article by Nancy Frey that appeared in *California English* (2003).

scaffold writing through the use of a pre-designed format. These writing frames, when paired with a picture book, are ideal for use in a writing course because the amount of text necessary to read is relatively short, allowing students to get down to the business of writing in short order.

Throughout the day, students move rapidly through these and other writing exercises designed to scaffold instruction that is related to their individual photo-essay books. Focused time for independent writing is also featured in each period. Using this instructional model, students average seventy minutes of writing—putting pen to paper—each day.

→ USING PICTURE BOOKS AS STORY FRAMES

In order to expose students to multiple story structures that might be useful in their photo essay project, we analyzed picture books that utilized visual information to augment written text. For example, we read the book *Beetle Boy* by Lawrence David, which was adapted from Kafka's novella *The Metamorphosis*. Although lacking the tragic ending of Kafka's original, *Beetle Boy* told the tale of a young boy named Gregory who awakens one morning to discover he's become a beetle. Much to his chagrin, no one seems to notice other than his best friend. We followed the reading with this RAFT writing frame:

R Gregory

A Mom and Dad

F Note

T Why don't you notice me?

During another class, we used *Fortunately* by Remy Charlip to present the simple plot device of using an alternating sequence of fortunate and unfortunate events to tell a cliffhanging adventure. In both instances, student writers extended the tales by writing a "next chapter" to follow where Charlip's story ended.

Other picture books presented in class as shared readings featured photographs to tell their stories and therefore aligned more explicitly with the requirements for the project. The next book we introduced was *Alex and Loki* by Charles Smith because it included photos in an alternating format (the perspectives of a boy and his dog) similar to the one used in *Fortunately.* These multiple writing opportunities prepared students to engage in their own creative writing project.

The works of William Wegman also were particularly well suited for this project. For nearly thirty years, Wegman has produced books featuring his beloved Weimaraner dogs in fanciful situations. *Surprise Party, Little Red Riding Hood*, and *My Town* were popular choices with the students, who could appreciate the sublime lunacy of dressing dogs for the purpose of telling funny stories. Wegman's books inspired Frederico to later write a spy novel starring his Chihuahua and pet hamster that owed much to Austin Powers and Wegman's dogs.

A final children's book used to model the assignment was *Stranger in the Woods* by Carl R. Sams and Jean Stoick. This beautifully photographed story tells the tale in poetic form of deer discovering a stranger—a snowman—and how they reconcile his presence in their domain. This story contributed to Edmundo's photo essay about a dog trying to understand what the boy with the camera was trying to do.

→ CONSTRUCTING A MODEL

We also constructed an original piece to model what we were looking for in this project. Using photographs we'd taken at a charity event, we wrote a fictional short story about crashing a celebrity party to meet famous guests. The story was fanciful enough to clearly be the product of our imaginations while at the same time featuring all of the elements necessary for the project. We used this opportunity to introduce the rubric that we created for this project using Web-based software (www.rubistar.com). A copy of our rubric can be found on page 144.

→ UP CLOSE: DEVELOPING A CREATIVE PHOTO ESSAY

Then it was time for students to storyboard their stories. They drew simple pictures to represent possible photos in a series of boxes and wrote text under each drawing. Some students had a very clear sense of what their stories would contain. Others were a bit more vague about their stories, with fewer cells and text planned.

At last the big day arrived—we distributed disposable cameras to each member of the class. They were instructed about the rules for using the 27 exposures—no photos in classrooms, always ask permission of those who are being photographed, and make sure your subject matter is appropriate for school. The first photo on the roll was to be of themselves so it could be used to identify developed film and it could be used at the end of the photo

RUBRIC FOR PHOTO ESSAY

Student Name: _____ Date: _____

Title: _____

CATEGORY	4	3	2	1
Required elements	Photo essay included all required elements as well as a few additional ones.	Photo essay included all required elements as well as one additional element.	Photo essay included all required elements.	One or more required elements were missing from the photo essay.
Spelling and grammar	Little or no spelling or grammatical mistakes on a photo essay with lots of text.	Little or no spelling or grammatical mistakes on a photo essay with less text.	Several spelling or grammatical mistakes on a photo essay with lots of text.	Several spelling or grammatical mistakes on a photo essay with little text.
Use of time	Used time well during each class period with no adult reminders.	Used time well during most class periods with no adult reminders.	Used time well but required adult reminders on one or more occasions.	Used time poorly in spite of several adult reminders.
Content	Photo essay uses both text and pictures to tell an imaginative story.	Photo essay uses mostly text, with some support from pictures, to tell an imaginative story.	Some pictures and text are not clearly related to one another.	Text and pictures have little connection with one another.

REQUIRED ELEMENTS:

- 15 to 20 photographs used in photo essay.
- Text is typed or written neatly.
- Photo essay includes a cover with title, author, and illustration.
- "About the Author" essay included.

essay for an "About the Author" page. After having their own pictures taken, they listened to descriptions of themselves that authors like Maya Angelou, Francisco Jimenez, and Sandra Cisneros had used in their books. Thus, the last page was written first as students composed this page in their writer's notebooks.

One week later, all the film had been developed and returned to the students. (Interestingly, three students supplemented their photo essays with pictures from magazines.) All the students mounted their photos on individual sheets of construction paper and then began rearranging the images into an order that would support a story. This was a critical phase of the project and proved to be more difficult for some students than others. While many had a skeleton of a story in mind before they began shooting their photos, others seemed a bit looser. Some students deviated very little from their original storyboards. On the other hand, there were students who had created a strong storyboard but discovered that they didn't have the quality shot they wanted to illustrate a page in their story. Those students usually altered their stories a bit to accommodate the photos they did have.

In all cases, we conferred with individual students as they orally constructed their stories. This proved to be invaluable because we could ask clarifying questions and discuss word choice, use of imagery, and plot devices.

Since many of these writers are English language learners, the use of oral composition before written composition allowed them to be more adventurous in the complexity of their writing. With some students, we used a modified Language Experience Approach to record their key story developments. Once a student had conferred with us, he or she began writing a first draft. When that draft was completed, students met individually with us to refine and edit their work. The checklist used to support a writer's conference appears on page 146. Work on this phase of the project continued for the next week.

→ GALLERY WALK: THE FINISHED PRODUCT

Two weeks after students had received their cameras, they were displaying their work in a Gallery Walk. A Gallery Walk gives writers time to answer questions about their work. We divided our class into writers and readers. The writers stood next to their photo essays, which were displayed on their desks. The readers moved from one display to the next, reading the photo essays and asking questions of the authors. Halfway through the period, they switched roles.

Student: _____ Date: _____ Draft # _____

CATEGORY	RESPONSIBILITIES
Conventions	❑ My paragraphs have more than one sentence. ❑ Each of my paragraphs has one main idea. ❑ I have used correct grammar. ❑ I have used correct punctuation. ❑ I have checked my spelling. ❑ I have not used capital letters incorrectly. ❑ My handwriting is legible.
Organization	❑ My introduction is interesting and inviting. ❑ The sequence of ideas is logical. ❑ My ideas flow from one to another. ❑ I use helpful transitions between main points, (e.g., *First of all*, or *Similarly*). ❑ I have a satisfying conclusion.
Flow	❑ My sentences build logically upon the one(s) before. ❑ My sentences are different lengths. ❑ My sentences start in different ways. ❑ There are no run-on sentences. ❑ There are no incomplete sentences.
Punctuation	❑ I use commas to separate items in a series. ❑ I place a comma after an introductory word or phrase. ❑ I use a semicolon to connect two sentences. ❑ I place closing quotation marks after commas or periods. ❑ I use apostrophes to show possession or to create contractions. ❑ I have checked that a period, question mark, or exclamation point ends every sentence.
Word Choice	❑ I use descriptive words (adjectives and adverbs) often. ❑ I use strong, active verbs. ❑ I use synonyms and different words to add variety. ❑ My pronouns match the nouns to which they refer.

Students engaged in this project with an unprecedented level of enthusiasm. We had some outstanding stories that represented an array of interests. There were stories based on themes related to hopes and dreams. For instance, Antwoine described amazing basketball exploits in "Adam Park Ballers" when he wrote about a swish shot that impressed female fans:

So at this point in the game the score is 30–0 and my team is hot right now. I take a wide open shot and of course kissed the net for the ladies.

In her story "The Winner," Elena's protagonist, a middle-aged woman named Maria, experiences an event many of us dream about.

Early in the morning Maria woke up as usual to do her chores in the house. She fixed lunch for her husband so it would be ready when he came home from work. While Maria was washing the dishes she got a phone call. A woman on the phone told her she had won $50,000!

Two other students utilized a version of the transformative experience they had read about in *Beetle Boy*—changing into another animal and portraying the world through the animal's eyes. Edmundo used the clever device of inserting himself into the story of a boy who awakens to discover that he's become a dog:

I saw a kid coming toward me. I wanted to run but I stayed there to see what would happen. The kid started taking some pictures of me because he was doing a project; he thought I was funny.

Still others used the assignment as a way to integrate their interests in action stories and video games by constructing elaborate tales about superheroes, evil villains, martial arts, and comic book violence. Minh used the video game *War Craft III* as a central element in a tournament between the champion and three worthy challengers (all toddlers in the photographs!). His writing is laced with terminology specific to his generation, including a Japanese comic strip card game and a Korean gaming term meaning "expert":

When it was Chris's turn he jumped right in to build his army to conquer mine and win the prize money. I could hear him muttering, "I'm going to beat him and get the money to buy some Yu-Gi-Oh cards." I tried my best, but could not beat the GoSu.

Frederico's spy thriller starring his pets began with the kidnapping of a top government official. Then he continued:

He is missing and we (myself and the FBI) think that the evil Kiki had something to do with it. We have picked a top agent to solve the case. Agent Boulder is his name and he's already investigating as we speak.

Perhaps the most poignant photo essays were those that could be described as realistic fiction. Xuan's story illustrated how violence can escalate rapidly from insignificant events when he described an argument over the superiority of video game systems that mushroomed into a gang fight:

They were all rumbling with each other, everyone against everyone. Henry was about to shoot, but the gun was out of bullets.

Like Frederico's story, Izabel's centered on a kidnapping, but hers had a dark tone. The protagonist called the authorities to report the crime but experiences a reality that people face in too many urban neighborhoods:

She rushed to the phone and called the police. They said they would be there in five minutes. They took two hours.

In all cases, the photos demonstrated the use of humor, drama, dialogue, and plot to advance the story.

→ CONCLUSION

We use a gradual-release model of writing to emphasize craft—mechanics, punctuation, word choice, and fluency—and to extend students' abilities to write coherently. After all, the power of a message can be lost in the chaos of poorly constructed sentences and paragraphs. However, efforts to accelerate skills development are wasted if the curriculum is not balanced with engaging and meaningful projects that encourage students to apply their growing proficiency in writing. The performance of our students in the photo essay project affirms that when given a task that allows students to express ideas using both visual and textual information, they will attend to the quality of their writing in order to enhance the images they have selected. By providing models, scaffolding portions of the writing in class, and conferring with writers as they develop their ideas, we give students the support they need to successfully complete the assignment.

Here's a final snapshot:

> The gallery walk of photo essays has inspired pride in the students, who are eager to share their work and see the final products of their classmates. The classroom has taken on a museum-like quality as students move from display to display, reading the print closely while examining the accompanying photographs. Antwoine turns to his teacher and asks, "What are we writing next?"

That's a picture worth a thousand words in any teacher's journal.

Background on Research

Support for independent writing has been widely touted in the literature. Lucy Calkins (1994) has written extensively about the role of listening to young writers to support the development of their ideas and drafts into products they find satisfying. Nancie Atwell (1998) has written eloquently about the lives of middle school students who use writing as a means to find their places in the world. Likewise, Janet Allen and Kyle Gonzalez (1998) have used their students' writing to teach us about our learners and ourselves. It seems that the field of independent writing in the classroom is rich with these kinds of ethnographic and qualitative studies that invite us all into the lives of students. Indeed, this is probably because young writers bare themselves to us through their writing each day. Therefore, we must see ourselves as stewards of their developing voices. We can accomplish this through curricular, collaborative, and coaching supports.

The role of background knowledge is critical to the quality of the written product (Marzano, 2004). This is especially evident in the types of reading students do to support their writing. Weih (2005) found that fifth-grade students who were instructed in narrative genres in reading adopted these elements in their independent writing. Bradley (2001) has written that even very young children are adept at providing viable feedback on writing for their peers. And student writers appear to profit from opportunities to interact with their peers during the development of their independent writing. In a study of fourth graders, Murphy (2003) found that students could support one another in learning specific approaches to the craft of writing. This distinction between mechanics and craft appears to be important. Lipson (2000) discovered that in classrooms where teachers emphasized conferences that centered on effective writing rather than conventions alone, writing improved, especially as it related to time sustained and ownership of ideas.

KEY POINTS
FOR THE LANGUAGE EXPERIENCE APPROACH LESSON

Independent writing projects give students an opportunity to consolidate background knowledge with more recently learned skills to explore various writing forms including summary writing, response to literature, technical documents, and persuasive essays. When launching an independent writing activity or project, keep the following information in mind:

- *Independent writing tasks are most effective when students see the tasks as purposeful and authentic.*

- *The skills and strategies needed to complete independent writing should be scaffolded at the word, sentence, and paragraph levels.*

- *Although it's called "independent writing," collaboration with the teacher and students' peers is vital for gaining useful feedback.*

References

INTRODUCTION

Cunningham, A. E., & Stanovich, K. E. (1998). What reading does for the mind. *American Educator, 22*(1-2) 8-15.

Fearn, L., & Farnan, N. (2001). *Interactions: Teaching writing and the language arts.* Boston: Houghton Mifflin.

Halliday, M. A. K. (1993). Toward a language-based theory of learning. *Linguistics and Education, 5,* 93-126.

Hayes, J. R. (2004). A new framework for understanding cognition and its effect in writing. In R. B. Ruddell, & N. J. Unrau (Eds.), *Theoretical Models and Processes of Reading* (5th ed., pp. 1399-1430). Newark, DE: International Reading Association.

Kaufer, D. S., Hayes, J. R., & Flower, L. S. (1986). Composing written sentences. *Research in the Teaching of English, 20,* 121-140.

Moore, K. (2002). An interview with Don Graves. *The California Reader, 35*(2), 50-53.

Shanahan, T. (1980). The impact of writing instruction on learning to read. *Reading World, 19,* 357-368.

CHAPTER 1

Ashton-Warner, S. (1963). *Teacher.* New York: Simon & Schuster.

Clark, L. (1974). *Can't read, can't write, can't talk too good either.* New York: Penguin.

Duke, N. K., & Pearson, P. D. (2004). Effective practices for developing reading comprehension. In A. Farstrup & J. Samuels (Eds.), *What research has to say about reading instruction* (3rd ed., pp. 205-242). Newark, DE: International Reading Association.

Dyson, A. H., & Freedman, S. W. (2003). Writing. In J. Flood, D. Lapp, J. R. Squire, & J. M. Jensen (Eds.), *Handbook of research on teaching the English language arts* (pp. 967-992). Mahwah, NJ: Lawrence Erlbaum.

Gibbons, P. (1991). *Learning to learn in a second language.* Portsmouth, NH: Heinemann.

Graves, M. F., & Graves, B. B. (2003). *Scaffolding reading experiences: Designs for student success* (2nd ed.). Norwood, MA: Christopher-Gordon.

CHAPTER 2

Brown, R. W. (1973). *A first language: The early stages.* Cambridge, MA: Harvard University Press.

Culham, R. (2003). *6 + 1 traits of writing: The complete guide grades 3 and up.* New York: Scholastic.

Kear, D. J., Coffman, G. A., McKenna, M. C., & Ambrosio, A. L. (2000). Measuring attitude toward writing: A new tool for teachers. *The Reading Teacher, 54,* 10-23.

Lapp D., & Flood, J. (2003). Understanding the learner: Using portable assessment. In R. L. McCormack & J. R. Paratore (Eds.), *After early intervention, then what? Teaching struggling readers in grades 3 and beyond* (pp. 10-24). Newark, DE: International Reading Association.

Simmons, J. (2003). Responders are taught, not born. *Journal of Adolescent & Adult Literacy, 46,* 684-693.

Spandel, V., & Stiggins, R. J. (1997). *Creating writers: Linking writing assessment and instruction* (2nd ed.). New York: Addison Wesley Longman.

CHAPTER 3

Ashton-Warner, S. (1963). *Teacher.* New York: Simon & Schuster.

Brehaut, L. (1994). Starting from scratch: Teaching an elderly man to read. *Good Practice in Australian Adult Literacy and Basic Education, 25,* 11-13, 15.

Britton, J. N., Burgess, T., Martin, N., McLeod, A., & Rosen, H. (1975). *The development of writing abilities, 11-18: Schools Council Project on written language of 11-18-year-olds.* London: Macmillan Education.

Clark, E. R. (1995). "How did you learn to write in English when you haven't been taught in English?": The language experience approach in a dual language program. *Bilingual Research Journal, 19,* 611-627.

Dixon, C., & Nessel, D. (1983). *Language experience approach to reading (and writing): Language-experience reading for second language learners.* Hayward, CA: Alemany.

Ewoldt, C., & Hammermeister, F. K. (1989). The language-experience approach to facilitating reading and writing for hearing-impaired students. *American Annals of the Deaf, 131,* 271-274.

Flood, J., & Lapp, D. (2000). Teaching writing in urban schools: Cognitive processes, curriculum resources, and the missing links—management and grouping. In R. Indrisano & J. R. Squire (Eds.), *Perspectives on writing: Research, theory, and practice* (pp. 233-250). Newark, DE: International Reading Association.

Gately, S. E. (2004). Developing concept of word. *Teaching Exceptional Children, 36*(6),16–22.

Gollub, M. (2000). *The Jazz Fly.* Santa Rosa, CA: Tortuga Press.

Karnowski, L. (1989). Using LEA with process writing. *The Reading Teacher, 42,* 462–465.

Lapp, D., Fisher, D., & Flood, J. (1999). Does it matter how you're grouped for instruction? Yes! Flexible grouping patterns promote student learning. *The California Reader, 33*(1), 28-32.

Lapp, D., Flood, J., & Goss, K. (2000). Desks don't move—students do: In effective classrooms. *The Reading Teacher, 54,* 31–36. An integrated approach to the teaching and assessment of language arts. In S. R. Hurley & J. V.

Tinajero (Eds.), *Literacy assessment of second language learners* (pp. 1-26). Boston: Allyn & Bacon.

Perez, S. A. (2000). Teaching second language learners in the regular classroom. *Reading Improvement, 37*(1), 45-48.

Purcell-Gates, V., & Waterman, R. (2000). *Now we read, we see, we speak: Portrait of literacy development in an adult Freirean-based class.* Mahwah, NJ: Lawrence Erlbaum Associates.

Sharp, S. J. (1989). Using content subject matter with LEA in middle school. *Journal of Reading, 33*(2), 108-112.

Stauffer, R. G. (1970). *The language experience approach to the teaching of reading.* New York: Harper & Row.

Winkler, H., & Oliver, L. (2003). *I got a D in salami.* New York: Grosset & Dunlap.

CHAPTER 4

Ashton-Warner, S. (1963). *Teacher.* New York: Simon & Schuster.

Button, K., Johnson, M. J., & Furgerson, P. (1996). Interactive writing in a primary classroom. *The Reading Teacher, 49*, 446-454.

Button, K., & Welton, D. (1997). Integrating literacy activities and social studies in the primary grades. *Social Studies and the Young Learner, 9*(4), 15-18.

Callella, T., & Jordano, K. (2002). *Interactive writing: Students and teachers 'sharing the pen' to create meaningful text.* Huntington Beach, CA: Creative Teaching Press.

Cannon, J. (1993). *Stellaluna.* San Diego, CA: Harcourt.

Clay, M. M. (2001). *Change over time in children's literacy development.* Portsmouth, NH: Heinemann.

Fisher, D., & Frey, N. (2002). Accelerating achievement for adolescent English language learners: Interactive writing grows up. *California English, 7*(4), 24-25.

Fisher, D., & Frey, N. (2003). Writing instruction for struggling adolescent readers: A gradual release model. *Journal of Adolescent and Adult Literacy, 46*, 396-405.

James, S. (1996). *Dear Mr. Blueberry.* New York: Aladdin.

Krull, K. (1994). *Lives of the writers: Comedies, tragedies (and what the neighbors thought).* New York: Harcourt.

McCarrier, A., Pinnell, G. S., & Fountas, I. C. (2000). *Interactive writing: How language and literacy come together, K-2.* Portsmouth, NH: Heinemann.

McKenzie, M. G. (1985). Shared writing: Apprenticeship in writing. *Language Matters, 1-2*, 1-5.

Pinnell, G. S., & McCarrier, A. (1994). Interactive writing: A transition tool for assisting children in learning to read and write. In E. Hiebert & B. Taylor (Eds.), *Getting reading right from the start: Effective early literacy interventions* (pp. 149-170). Needham Heights, MA: Allyn & Bacon.

Vygotsky, L. S. (1962). *Thought and language*. Cambridge, MA: MIT Press.

Vygotsky, L. S. (1978). *Mind in society: The development of higher psychological processes*. Cambridge, MA: Harvard University Press.

CHAPTER 5

LaBerge, D., & Samuels, S. A. (1974). Toward a theory of automatic information processing in reading. *Cognitive Psychology, 6*, 293–323.

Elbow, P. (1981). *Writing with power: Techniques for mastering the writing process.* New York: Oxford University Press.

Fearn, L., & Farnan, N. (2001). *Interactions: Teaching writing and the language arts*. Boston: Houghton Mifflin.

Fisher, D., Frey, N., Farnan, N., Fearn, L., & Petersen, F. (2004). Increasing writing achievement in an urban middle school. *Middle School Journal, 36*(2), 21–26.

Hayes, J. B., & Flower, L. S. (1980). Writing as problem solving. *Visible Language, 14*, 388-399.

Kasper-Ferguson, S., & Moxley, R. A. (2002). Developing a writing package with student graphing of fluency. *Education and Treatment of Children, 25*, 249-267.

Rasinski, T. V. (2003). *The fluent reader: Oral reading strategies for building word recognition, fluency, and comprehension.* New York: Scholastic.

White, E. B. (1974). *Charlotte's web*. New York: HarperTrophy.

CHAPTER 6

Dorn, L. J., & Soffos, C. (2001). *Scaffolding young writers: A writers' workshop approach.* Portland, ME: Stenhouse.

Enginarlar, H. (1994). Sentence combining plus: A new use for an old technique. *English Language Teachers Journal, 48*, 214-224.

Fearn, L., & Farnan, N. (2001). *Interactions: Teaching writing and the language arts*. Boston: Houghton Mifflin.

Fisher, D., & Frey, N. (2003). Writing instruction for struggling adolescent readers: A gradual release model. *Journal of Adolescent and Adult Literacy, 46*, 396-405.

Frey, N., & Fisher, D. (2006). *The language arts workshop: Purposeful reading and writing instruction*. Upper Saddle River, NJ: Merrill Prentice Hall.

Herrell, A. L. (2000). *Fifty strategies for teaching English language learners*. Upper Saddle River, NJ: Merrill Prentice Hall.

Kear, D. J., Coffman, G. A., McKenna, M. C., & Ambrosio, A. L. (2000). Measuring attitude toward writing: A new tool for teachers. *The Reading Teacher, 54*, 10-23.

Manning, M. M., Manning, G. L., & Long, R. (1995). Development of kindergartners' ideas about what is written in a written sentence. *Journal of Research in Childhood Education, 10*, 29-36.

McAfee, D. C. (1980). *Effect of sentence-combining instruction on the reading and writing achievement of fifth-grade children in a suburban school district.* Unpublished doctoral dissertation, Texas Woman's University, Denton.

Mellon, J. C. (1969). *Transformational sentence-combining: A method for enhancing the development of syntactic fluency in English compositions.* Urbana, IL: National Council of Teachers of English.

O'Hare, F. (1973). *Sentence combining: Improving student writing without formal grammar instruction.* Urbana, IL: National Council of Teachers of English.

Parkes, B. (2000). *Read it again! Revisiting shared reading.* York, ME: Stenhouse.

Saddler, B., & Graham, S. (2005). The effects of peer-assisted sentence-combining instruction on the performance of more and less skilled young writers. *Journal of Educational Psychology, 97*(1), 43-54.

CHAPTER 7

Azarian, M. (2000). *A gardener's alphabet.* Boston: Houghton Mifflin.

Calfee, R., Chambliss, M., & Beretz, M. (1991). Organizing for comprehension and composition. In W. Ellis (Ed.), *All language and the creation of literacy* (pp. 79-93). Baltimore: Orton Dyslexia Society.

Charlip, R. (1993). *Fortunately.* New York: Scott Foresman.

Charney, D. H., & Carlson, R. A. (1995). Learning to write in a genre: What student writers take from model texts. *Research in the Teaching of English, 29*, 88-125.

Creech, S. (2001). *Love that dog.* New York: HarperCollins.

Cunningham, J. (1982). Generating interactions between schema and text. In J. A. Niles & I. A. Harris (Eds.), *New inquiries in reading research and instruction* (pp. 42-47). Washington, D.C.: National Reading Conference.

Erikson, P. (1997). *Daily life in a covered wagon.* New York: Penguin.

Fisher, D., & Drake, L. (1999). Connecting geometry to students' experiences. In S. Totten, C. Johnson, L. R. Morrow, T. Sills-Briegel (Eds.), *Practicing what we preach: Preparing middle level educators* (pp. 128-131). New York: Falmer.

Greene, B. G. (1994). Assessing literacy: Writing models, portfolios, & performances. *Reading Research and Instruction, 33*, 257-262.

Koch, K. (1997). I never told anybody: Four poetry writing ideas. *Teachers & Writers, 29*, 1-10.

Levitin, S. (2000). *Dream freedom.* San Diego: Silver Whistle/Harcourt.

Martinez, V. (1996). *Parrot in the oven: Mi Vida.* New York: Joanna Cotler.

McElveen, S. A., & Dierking, C. C. (2000/2001). Children's books as models to teach writing skills. *The Reading Teacher, 54*, 362-364.

Moretti, C. (1996). *Literary creativity with art: A resource teacher project.* La Mesa, CA: Grossmont Union High School District.

Oja, L. A. (1996). Using story frames to develop reading comprehension. *Journal of Adolescent & Adult Literacy, 40*, 129-130.

Pearson, P. D., & Gallagher, M. C. (1983). The instruction of reading comprehension. *Contemporary Educational Psychology, 8*, 317-344.

Shannon, D. (1998). *A bad case of the stripes*. New York: Blue Sky Press.

Sipe, L. R. (1993). Using transformations of traditional stories: Making the reading-writing connection. *The Reading Teacher, 47*, 18-26.

Staal, L. A. (2001). Writing models: Strategies for writing composition in inclusive settings. *Reading & Writing Quarterly, 17*, 243-248.

Thomas, S. M. (1998). *Somewhere today: A book of peace*. Morton Grove, IL: Albert Whitman & Co.

Tompkins, G. E. (1990). *Teaching writing: Balancing process and product*. New York: Macmillan Publishing.

CHAPTER 8

Allen, J., & Gonzalez, K. (1998). *There's room for me here: Literacy workshop in the middle school*. Stenhouse: York, ME.

Angelou, M. (1983). *I know why the caged bird sings*. New York: Bantam.

Atwell, N. (1998). *In the middle: New understanding about writing, reading, and learning* (2nd ed.). Portsmouth, NH: Boynton/Cook.

Barone, D. M., & Taylor, J. (2006). *Improving students' writing, K-8: From meaning making to high stakes!* Thousand Oaks, CA: Corwin.

Bradley, D. H. (2001). How beginning writers demonstrate their understanding of the act of writing. *Reading Research and Instruction, 40*, 273-296.

Calkins, L. M. (1994). *The art of teaching writing*. Portsmouth, NH: Heinemann.

Charlip, R. (1993). *Fortunately*. New York: Scott Foresman.

David, L. (1999). *Beetle boy*. Dragonfly.

Frank, A. (1993). *Anne Frank: The diary of a young girl*. New York: Bantam.

Frey, N. (2003). A picture prompts a thousand words: Creating photo essays with struggling writers. *California English, 8*(5), 16-21.

Hammond, B. (1998). Time to reassess the application essay. *Journal of College Admission,161*, 3-4.

Kafka, F. (1972). *The metamorphosis*. New York: Bantam.

Lipson, M. Y., Mosenthal, J., & Daniels, P. (2000). Process writing in the classrooms of eleven fifth-grade teachers with different orientations to teaching and learning. *The Elementary School Journal, 101*, 209-231.

Lowry, L. (1998). *Number the stars*. New York: Laurel Leaf.

Marzano, R. J. (2004). *Building background knowledge for academic achievement: Research on what works in schools*. Alexandria, VA: Association for Supervision and Curriculum Development.

McCourt, F. (2005). *Teacher man: A memoir*. New York: Scribner.

Mooney, J., & Cole, D. (2000). *Learning outside the lines*. New York: Simon & Schuster.

Murphy, P. (2003). Discovering the ending in the beginning. *Language Arts, 80,* 461-469.

Patterson, S. (2005). How much is too much? Ethical and effective response to the application essay. *Journal of College Admission,189,* 2-5.

Santa, C., & Havens, L. (1995). *Creating independence through student-owned strategies: Project CRISS.* Dubuque, IA: Kendall-Hunt.

Smith, C. R., Jr. (2001). *Loki and Alex: The adventures of a dog and his best friend.* New York: Dutton.

Wegman, W. (1998). *My town.* New York: Hyperion.

Wegman, W. (1999). *Little red riding hood.* New York: Hyperion.

Wegman, W. (2000). *Surprise party.* New York: Hyperion.

Weih, G. (2005). The genre of traditional literature influences in student writing. *Reading Horizons, 46*(2), 77-91.

Wiesner, D. (1991). *Tuesday.* New York: Clarion.

Wong, H. K., & Wong, R. T. (2001). *The first days of school: How to be an effective teacher.* Mountain View, CA: Harry K. Wong.

Yolen, J. (1990). *The devil's arithmetic.* New York: Puffin.

Index